T0381912

Cambridge Elements ≡

Elements in Corpus Linguistics
edited by
Susan Hunston
University of Birmingham

PROGRAMMING FOR CORPUS LINGUISTICS WITH PYTHON AND DATAFRAMES

Daniel Keller
Western Kentucky University

CAMBRIDGE
UNIVERSITY PRESS

CAMBRIDGE
UNIVERSITY PRESS

Shaftesbury Road, Cambridge CB2 8EA, United Kingdom

One Liberty Plaza, 20th Floor, New York, NY 10006, USA

477 Williamstown Road, Port Melbourne, VIC 3207, Australia

314–321, 3rd Floor, Plot 3, Splendor Forum, Jasola District Centre,
New Delhi – 110025, India

103 Penang Road, #05-06/07, Visioncrest Commercial, Singapore 238467

Cambridge University Press is part of Cambridge University Press & Assessment,
a department of the University of Cambridge.

We share the University's mission to contribute to society through the pursuit of
education, learning and research at the highest international levels of excellence.

www.cambridge.org
Information on this title: www.cambridge.org/9781009486781

DOI: 10.1017/9781108904094

© Daniel Keller 2024

When citing this work, please include a reference to the DOI 10.1017/9781108904094

First published 2024

A catalogue record for this publication is available from the British Library.

ISBN 978-1-009-48678-1 Hardback
ISBN 978-1-108-82258-9 Paperback
ISSN 2632-8097 (online)
ISSN 2632-8089 (print)

Additional resources for this publication at www.cambridge.org/Keller

Programming for Corpus Linguistics with Python and Dataframes

Elements in Corpus Linguistics

DOI: 10.1017/9781108904094
First published online: May 2024

Daniel Keller
Western Kentucky University
Author for correspondence: Daniel Keller, daniel.keller@wku.edu

Abstract: This Element offers intermediate or experienced programmers algorithms for Corpus Linguistic (CL) programming in the Python language using dataframes that provide a fast, efficient, intuitive set of methods for working with large, complex datasets such as corpora. This Element demonstrates principles of dataframe programming applied to CL analyses, as well as complete algorithms for creating concordances; producing lists of collocates, keywords, and lexical bundles; and performing key feature analysis. An additional algorithm for creating dataframe corpora is presented including methods for tokenizing, part-of-speech tagging, and lemmatizing using spaCy. This Element provides a set of core skills that can be applied to a range of CL research questions, as well as to original analyses not possible with existing corpus software.

Keywords: corpus linguistics, programming, Python, corpus linguistic methods, algorithms for corpus linguistics

ISBNs: 9781009486781 (HB), 9781108822589 (PB), 9781108904094 (OC)
ISSNs: 2632-8097 (online), 2632-8089 (print)

Contents

1 Dataframe Corpora

This Element is about programming for corpus linguistics using dataframes – that is, storing linguistic data in a table with a small number of columns and many rows and then using that table to facilitate corpus linguistic analyses. This allows the analyst to do things like create concordances, find lists of collocates, and produce per-text frequency counts of linguistic features quickly and efficiently.

In addition, this Element contains a general introduction to the Python programming language focusing on working with text data, as well as a basic introduction to writing algorithms. This is not, however, an introduction to corpus linguistics (hereafter, CL) or programming more generally. This Element is written under the assumption that readers are familiar with CL concepts such as corpora, collocation, and normalized frequency, and have some experience writing scripts in Python or another programming language.

1.1 The Dataframe Approach to CL Programming

A dataframe corpus is a single table that contains the complete text and metadata of a corpus. Each row corresponds to one token from one text. The columns hold distinct types of information about those tokens. One column typically contains the word itself (e.g., *and*) while others contain metadata. This may be part-of-speech (POS) tags (e.g., *CC* for *coordinating conjunction*), the ID number of the text the token is drawn from, a speaker or author ID, and so on.

Using dataframe corpora simplifies the programming involved in CL tasks. Dataframes provide a set of powerful tools for things like counting values in a column, grouping rows, and applying mathematical formulae. If an analyst wants to know the number of times each word in a dataframe corpus appears, they need only load the corpus from disk and count the values in the token column. These two tasks can be accomplished with two instructions, typically in a matter of seconds.

1.1.1 The Pandas Package

While some other programming languages have tools for manipulating and analyzing data in tables, Python does not. Consequently, it is necessary to install additional software to work with dataframes effectively. In this Element, we will use a software package called Pandas for this purpose.

1.1.2 A Note on Formatting

Throughout this Element, the names of keywords, methods, functions, properties, and variables are presented in a monospace font. This is to distinguish elements of code from the language used to describe them. For example, in the sentence "`import` is used to import packages," the first instance of "import" is presented in monospace to indicate that it is a Python keyword, while the second is a verb describing its use. Similarly, when a word like *dataframe* is presented as code (e.g., `DataFrame`), it refers to Pandas `DataFrames`, and when it is not, it refers to the concept of a dataframe more generally (i.e., a tabular data structure).

1.2 Who Is This Element For?

This Element is written for analysts who have some familiarity with programming. Students who have taken a course in a programming language and who are looking for techniques specifically for corpus linguistic analysis will find this Element useful, as will established researchers who want to make their coding more efficient or their approach more systematic.

For beginners, this Element will work best in conjunction with a more fully fledged Python textbook. Section 2 provides a brief introduction to the Python language. However, that section is designed to provide just enough Python to get the reader to Section 3, and some readers may need to consult other sources to learn more about the Python language.

1.3 Advantages of Using Dataframes

1.3.1 Fewer Things to Learn

Programming with dataframes involves using a small set of processes such as filtering and counting to perform complex manipulations of the underlying data. Tasks in CL can be accomplished by combining these processes.

1.3.2 Faster Development

With dataframes, many tasks can be accomplished in just a few lines of code. Writing less code means shorter development times, fewer opportunities to make mistakes, and less time spent debugging.

1.3.3 Chainable Output

Processes performed on dataframes often produce other dataframes. This allows functions and algorithms to be chained together so that one CL task (e.g., creating *n*-grams) can be chained directly into other tasks (e.g., counting values).

1.3.4 Memory Efficiency

Dataframes require less memory to hold large amounts of data than do other data structures. This allows analysts to work with larger corpora.

1.3.5 Execution Speed

Many of Pandas' `DataFrame` tools are implemented in a way that makes them extremely fast in comparison to Python scripts that do not use dataframes.

1.3.6 Vector-Based Operations

Dataframes allow computation on entire vectors (i.e., a sequence or list) at one time – for example, multiplying each element in a sequence by a number without cycling through the sequence.

1.3.7 Transfer

A dataframe created in Python can be imported into other languages like R, or into spreadsheet software like Excel or Google Sheets. Similarly, the principles of dataframe programming transfer to other programming languages as well.

1.3.8 Interactivity

The combination of these characteristics makes dataframes an ideal datatype for working with Python's interpreter interactively (through, e.g., iPython, Jupyter, or IDLE).

1.4 What Is in This Element?

Section 1 contains an introduction to the Element and the corpus used through-out. Section 2 reviews some of the basics of programming in Python. Section 3 describes the dataframe approach to CL programming by introducing a core set of techniques for manipulating Pandas `DataFrames`. Methods for loading, examining, and writing dataframes to disk are explained, as are methods for filtering and locating rows of interest, and for working with larger segments of the corpus than individual tokens. In the fourth section, algorithms for a range of common CL tasks are introduced: creating a concordance, identifying lexical bundles, generating a list of collocates, finding keywords, and performing key feature analysis. The algorithms in Section 4 are designed to demonstrate various approaches to CL analysis that can be extended to a range of other uses. Finally, in the fifth section, an algorithm for creating dataframe corpora from text files is explained. This section also covers tokenizing, part-of-speech tagging, and lemmatizing using the spaCy library for Natural Language Processing.

1.4.1 The Corpus of Online Registers of English (CORE)

The code in this Element makes use of the Corpus of Online Registers of English (CORE; Biber & Egbert, 2018). The Element employs CORE for both technical and linguistic reasons. First, CORE has been used in dozens of peer-reviewed studies in register variation and natural language processing. It is an established corpus with an active user base. Using CORE in examples and making the corpus available for download as a dataframe ensure that readers will have a corpus they may use in their own research. Second, CORE includes texts from a range of online registers, and these registers can be treated as subcorpora. Consequently, procedures that typically require multiple corpora (e.g., keyword analysis) can be demonstrated with a single corpus. Additionally, this register diversification allows analysts to compare the use of linguistic features within or across situations of use. Basic descriptive statistics of the corpus are presented in Table 1.

The corpus has been converted to a Pandas DataFrame for the exercises in this Element. This dataframe contains seven columns described in Table 2.

The dataframe version of CORE can be downloaded at www.cambridge.org/Keller or https://sites.google.com/view/programming-for-cl/home.

1.4.2 A Note on Operating Systems

Python is platform independent; Python code can be executed on any computer with an operating system that has a Python interpreter. This means that while the code in this Element was written on a computer running Microsoft Windows, most of the code will work on MacOS as well. However, due to differences in the file structures of the two operating systems, some adjustment may be necessary.

Table 1 Descriptive statistics for CORE

Statistic	Value
Number of tokens (including punctuation)	69,933,607
Number of words (excluding punctuation)	60,929,959
Number of word types	355,836
Number of texts	48,571

Table 2 Columns in the CORE dataframe

Column name	Type of data contained in that column
token	The token from the original CORE file
type	The fully lowercase form of the token
lemma	The base form of the token without inflectional morphemes
tag	The Penn Treebank POS tag
pos	The Universal Dependency Project POS tag (Nivre et al., 2017)
text	The CORE ID number of the text the token is from
register	The CORE register category of the text

2 Python Basics for Corpus Linguistics

2.1 Installing Python

Installing Python involves two steps:

1. installing a Python interpreter, and
2. adding the directory where the Python interpreter is installed to your system path.

The second step is not necessary, but many guides will assume you have done this. In addition to the basic installation, it may be a good idea to download and install an integrated development environment (IDE) such as PyCharm or Spyder. For the sake of brevity, this Element will not cover the installation process. It is documented at www.python.org/downloads/.

2.2 Python Versions

Two major versions of Python are in use at the time of writing: Python 2 and Python 3. Python 3 is the currently in-development version of the language, while Python 2 is maintained for backward compatibility. All code demonstrated in this Element is written for compatibility with Python 3.11. Any version of the Python interpreter greater than or equal to 3.11 should be able to execute all code in this Element.

2.3 Using IDLE

The Python interpreter comes bundled with IDLE (Integrated Development and Learning Environment). As the name suggests, IDLE is an excellent environment for learning the ins and outs of the Python language. The IDLE interface allows you to type commands directly into the interpreter and see the results immediately. The code in the following sections can be executed in IDLE.

2.4 Data and Operations

Programming often involves manipulating data. In CL, our data are samples of language, and our operations are things like counting word types, calculating association strength, measuring dispersion, and so on. To accomplish these things, we need to be able to hold and reference data in a computer's memory, often in discrete chunks. We do this with variables. To perform operations on these variables, we write instructions (code) that the Python interpreter understands how to carry out. We can group sets of instructions and save them to be reused later. These are called functions. Often, we will use functions written by other people to save time and guarantee replicability.

2.5 Variables

If we want to work with data (and we do), we need a name for that data. By assigning data to a variable and giving it a name, we tell the Python interpreter that this chunk of information is something we want to keep and reuse and that we want to call it by the name we have given it. Variable names in Python can be any sequence of characters that starts with a letter (or the underscore character _) and that does not include any of Python's reserved words. Variable names in Python are typically descriptive of the type of information they hold. There are conventions for naming variables, but so long as you are writing code for yourself and do not expect others to maintain or extend it, the conventions are not critically important.

We create variables and assign data to them in a single step by using the = operator.

```
greeting = 'hello world'
```

creates a variable called `greeting` and assigns the value *hello world* to it. If we are working with the interpreter directly (for example, if you are using IDLE) and if we want to see the value of a variable, we can just type its name (if you are using a different application [e.g., PyCharm or Spyder], you may need to save the preceding code in a .py file and execute it to see the results).

```
greeting
```

```
'hello world'
```

In the code we have just executed, we enclosed the greeting message in quotation marks.

```
greeting = 'hello world'
```

We did this to tell Python that the variable contains a type of data called a *string*. Strings are a datatype. There are many types of data and corresponding Python datatypes. Understanding the differences is very important.

2.6 Datatypes

Imagine sitting down to lunch. You have prepared a grilled cheese sandwich, tomato soup, and coffee. You likely have three pieces of dinnerware in front of you, a plate for the sandwich, a bowl for the soup, and a mug for the coffee. This arrangement is fairly fixed. You could put the sandwich in the bowl, but putting the soup on the plate is a bad idea. You might put the soup in the cup, but putting coffee in the bowl would make drinking it a frustrating experience.

Just as there are types of dinnerware for types of food, there are types of variables for types of data. In Python, `int` variables hold integers (whole, real numbers, positive or negative); `float` variables hold numbers with values other than 0 to the right of a decimal point; `char` variables hold single characters (e.g., a, 5, ?); `str` (string) variables hold sequences of characters (e.g., `'hello world'`); `lists` hold multiple other variables in a fixed order (e.g., a `list` of strings); `dicts` (dictionaries) hold key/value pairs, where looking up the key returns the value just as you might look up a word in a dictionary to get its definition. You can find out what datatype a variable is with the `type()` function. To check the datatype of `greeting` in the code we executed earlier, we use

```
type(greeting)
```

str

and we see the datatype of `greeting` is `str`.

Variable datatypes are important because they define what you can do with data. You can add two integers.

```
a = 4
b = 5
a + b
```

9

But, if you add two strings 'hello' and 'world',

```
a = 'hello'
b = 'world'
a + b
```

'helloworld'

you get a single concatenated string 'helloworld.' There is no space between hello and world because we did not add it. We could.

```
a + ' ' + b
```

'hello world'

The same holds for numbers that are stored as strings. If you add the strings '4' and '5', you get '45,' not '9.' If you add two lists, the second list is appended to the end of the first. If you add two dictionaries, or a string and an integer, you get an error.

Variables can be converted from one datatype to another with the name of the datatype followed by the variable to convert in parentheses. For example,

```
str(a)
```

converts the variable *a* to a string. Some variables cannot be converted directly between types. The string '35' can be converted to the integer 35, but "thirty-five" cannot.

2.7 Methods and Properties

Python datatypes have code for handling common tasks built right in. For example, strings have a way to count the number of times another string appears in them. If you type

```
greeting.count('world')
```

1

Python returns 1 because the string 'world' appears one time in 'hello world' (the value of `greeting`). This is called a string method because it can be invoked on any string. We can also access the methods of most datatypes through literal examples of that type. For example, instead of assigning 'hello world' to a variable, we could just type

```
'hello world'.count('world')
```

1
Here, 'hello world' is called a string literal. We will see `list` literals and `dict` literals later.

The `count ()` method is of the `str` (string) datatype, but datatypes also have properties, or metadata, associated with them. Variables of the `int` datatype, for example, have a property called `denominator`. When this property is invoked, Python returns the denominator of the value of the variable. A variable's methods and properties together are called its attributes.

2.8 Accessing Attributes with the Dot Operator

To access the properties and methods of a datatype, you type a `.` after either the name of the datatype, or a variable of that datatype's name. The `.` here is called the dot operator. After the `.`, you can type the name of the method or property to access it. We previously used the dot operator to access the `count ()` method of the `str` datatype. We can also use it to access the denominator property of the `int` type.

```
num = 5
num.denominator
```

1
Python returns 1 because the denominator of any integer is one.

2.9 Invoking Methods

Methods differ from properties in that when they are accessed, a set of instructions is executed. Sometimes, these methods require additional information to work. We can give the method the information it needs in parentheses after the name of the method. Earlier, we used the string method `count ()`.

First, we assigned the value 'hello world' to the variable `greeting` using the `=` operator. Next, we counted the occurrences of `'world'` in `greeting` and got 1. The `count ()` method requires additional information to work – what to count. We tell `count ()` what to count in parentheses after the name of the method. This is called "passing a variable into the method." The value that we pass into the method is called an argument. We can describe what happens in the second line by saying we invoked the `count ()` method of the string variable `greeting` and passed the string `'world'` into the method for its argument.

Note that when we refer to the `count ()` method, we include parentheses. This indicates that we are referring to a method (or function – more on functions in a moment). Names without trailing parentheses refer to variables, properties, or keywords, while names with trailing parentheses refer to methods or functions.

2.10 Calling Functions

Functions are called just like methods, by typing their names and passing any information needed into the function as arguments. Unlike methods, however, functions do not need to be invoked on a variable or datatype. Consequently, methods tend to work in ways that are idiosyncratic for the datatype for which they are an attribute. Functions, on the other hand, are more general.

We have used one function already, `type()`.

```
type(greeting)
```

is syntax for calling the `type()` function on the variable `greeting`.

2.11 Defining Functions

Programmers often need to write sets of instructions that they can apply repeatedly to different variables; that is, they need to write their own functions. In Python, we do this by using the `def` keyword. Keywords have special meaning in Python (they may start a loop or block of code or tell Python to execute one set of instructions under one condition and another set under a different condition). The `def` keyword creates a function that can be called later in the program. It is always followed by a name for the function, a set of parentheses, and a colon. The names of variables the function will need to access should be included in the parentheses. If no variables are needed, the parentheses should remain empty. The instructions come after the `def` statement and are indented one level.

```
def count_vowels(text):
    text = text.lower()
    num = text.count('a')
    num = num + text.count('e')
    num = num + text.count('i')
    num = num + text.count('o')
    num = num + text.count('u')
    return num
result = count_vowels('I think pugs are lazy animals.')
result
```

9

In the preceding code, we define a function called `count_vowels()` and tell the function to expect a variable called `text`. In the function, we invoke another string method, `lower()`, on the variable `text`. This method takes the value of the variable and converts it to lowercase. In the same line, we assign the output of the `lower()` method to the original variable `text`. This replaces the value we passed in, but without this assignment, we would lose the new lowercase values into the void. We then use the count () string method to count five vowel types, each time adding the number to the current value of num. Finally, we send the value of num back out of the function using the return keyword. The result is the number of times the five vowels occur in text.

2.12 Return Values, Return Types, and *None*

Every function in Python returns something after it is called. In the preceding example, the function count_vowels() returns an integer. As noted earlier, we can take that return value and assign it to a variable of our choosing by using the assignment operator =. The value returned by count_vowels() is stored in a new variable result.

The count () and count_vowels() methods return int variables. The lower() method and its opposite upper() return str variables. They have different return types. Some functions and methods appear not to return anything, however. In these cases, they return a special Python datatype called None. No data is associated with None, but Python still recognizes None as a value. You can assign None to a variable using =, and if you print the variable name, you will see nothing. If you check its type, Python will tell you NoneType.

2.13 Chaining Methods

If you know the type of data that a method returns, you can access the methods and properties of the return type by typing a . after the method invocation. We know, for example, that lower() returns a string. So, we can chain the output from lower() into another str method like count () without assigning the output of lower() to a variable first. You can also invoke methods on variables as you pass them into a method or function. Both techniques tell Python to do A and then do B with the result of A.

```
'THIS IS A SENTENCE.'.lower().count('is')
```

2

Since what we care about is the count, not the intermediate variables (the lowercased string), this gets to what we care about without the extraneous variables. Chaining in this way can also make code more readable since readers will not need to keep track of the values of unimportant variables. It can also make code *less* readable; however, if the chaining becomes too extensive or if the return values of the intermediate methods are difficult to discern. We will use chaining, but we will keep the number of functions chained to around three.

2.14 More on Lists and Dictionaries

Lists and dictionaries hold instances of other values or variables. Dictionaries hold pairs of values (called *items*) where the first is the key and the second is the value. If you know the key, you can look up the value. Lists are useful, but working with them can be resource-intensive and slow. Dictionaries are faster and often easier to work with when data can be stored as key/value pairs.

2.14.1 Working with Lists

Consider the following code.

```
beginning = 'It was a dark and stormy night'
words = beginning.split()
words
```

```
['It', 'was', 'a', 'dark', 'and', 'stormy', 'night']
```
In this example, we first assign the value `'It was a dark and stormy night.'` to a variable we have named `beginning`. In the next line, we invoke the `split()` string method on `beginning` and assign the return value to a new variable, `words`. `split()` is a string method that takes the value of the string and splits it at every occurrence of one or more characters. By default, strings are split on whitespace characters (the characters created by pressing the space bar, return/enter, or tab). However, you may change this behavior by passing different characters into the method (by including them in the parentheses).

The return value of `split()` is a list containing all the substrings that resulted from the split. Since we had a space between each word, the resulting list contains all the words in `beginning`.

In Python, `list` variables are denoted using square brackets `[]`. The elements in the list are separated from each other with commas. Further, in the preceding example, we can see that each element in the list is a `str` variable because they are enclosed in quotation marks. We can create a `list` literal using this same notation.

```
ending = ['and', 'they', 'all', 'lived', 'happily',
'ever', 'after']
type(ending)
```

```
list
```

2.14.2 Joining Elements in Lists

Just as there is a `str` method that converts a `str` to a `list`, there is a complementary method that joins a `list` of `str` variables into a single string, `join()`.

```
' '.join(ending)
```

`'and they all lived happily ever after'`

Since this is a `str` method, we invoke it on the string. Whatever string we use here is interspersed among the elements of the list.

```
'^_^'.join(ending)
```

`'and^_^they^_^all^_^lived^_^happily^_^ever^_^after'`

2.14.3 Accessing Elements in Lists

We can access an element of a `list` with its index using square brackets.

```
words[4]
```

`'and'`

Note that and is the fifth word in `beginning`, not the fourth. In Python, lists are 0-based (or 0-indexed). This means Python starts counting the elements in the list at 0, rather than 1. The elements of `words` with their indices are shown in Table 3.

If you ask Python how many elements are in the list though, it will provide the expected answer.

```
len(words)
```

`7`

The `len()` function returns an integer for the number of elements in a `list` or `dict`, or the number of characters in a string.

2.14.4 List Slicing

You can access a sublist (or slice) of a `list` using square brackets with a `:` separating the index of the first element and the index of the last element in the desired sublist + 1. This is called list slicing. The return type is also a `list`.

```
words[2:4]
```

Table 3 Indexed
elements of words

Index	Element
0	It
1	Was
2	A
3	Dark
4	And
5	Stormy
6	Night

```
['a', 'dark']
```
Note that the sublist contains only elements 2 and 3 of words, not 4. This is because Python is a 0-based language. Since we start counting at 0, we stop counting one number below the second index. Thus, the length of the returned list (2) is equal to the second index (4) minus the first (2). When the desired slice starts at the beginning of the list, the first element can be dropped.

```
words[:4]
```
```
['It', 'was', 'a', 'dark']
```
When the desired slice ends at the end of the list, you can drop the second index.

```
words[2:]
```
```
['a', 'dark', 'and', 'stormy', 'night']
```
It is possible to access the last element in a list with -1. This is an effective way to get the last *n* elements in a list when you are not sure how long the list is.

```
words[-1]
```
```
'night'
```

```
words[-4:]
```
```
['dark', 'and', 'stormy', 'night']
```

2.14.5 Appending to, Removing from, Copying, and Extending Lists

We can add elements to a list using the append() method.

```
words.append('.')
words
```

['It', 'was', 'a', 'dark', 'and', 'stormy', 'night', '.']
The append() method does not return a new list with the appended value.
Rather, it modifies the original list and returns None.

```
new_list = words.append('.')
type(new_list)
```

NoneType
It is also worth noting that we have appended a period, a punctuation mark, and
now the name of our list is a bit misleading as it contains both words and
punctuation. It is important to keep in mind that the name of a list has no bearing
on what it contains. Let us rename the list from words to tokens.

```
tokens = words.copy()
tokens
```

['It', 'was', 'a', 'dark', 'and', 'stormy', 'night', '.', '.']
Whoops! We have added two periods to the end of words (once with words.
append('.') and once with new_list = words.append('.'). We need
to get rid of one of those periods. We will use the remove() built-in method of
list variables. remove() looks for the first instance of an element in a list and
removes it.

```
words.remove('.')
words
```

['It', 'was', 'a', 'dark', 'and', 'stormy', 'night', '.']
Now, we will copy words again and store the new copy in the variable tokens.
While we are at it, we will use the extend function to add all the words from
ending to the same list. The extend() function is a built-in method of
list variables that takes a list as an argument and concatenates it to the end of
the first list. All the values of the second list (the one passed into the
method) are appended to the end of the list that extend() is invoked on.

```
tokens = words.copy()
tokens.extend(ending)
tokens
```

```
['It',
 'was',
 'a',
 'dark',
 'and',
 'stormy',
 'night',
 '.',
 'and',
 'they',
 'all',
 'lived',
 'happily',
 'ever',
 'after']
```

It is also possible to simply add the two lists together using the + operator.

```
tokens = words + ending
tokens
```

```
['It',
 'was',
 'a',
 'dark',
 'and',
 'stormy',
 'night',
 '.',
 'and',
 'they',
 'all',
 'lived',
 'happily',
 'ever',
 'after']
```

You may wonder whether it is possible to copy a list using the assignment operator =. While it is possible just to set `tokens` to equal `words` this way, doing so will link `tokens` to `words` so that any changes made to either will be reflected in the other. Essentially, we will have two names for the same data. If we want to copy a list as a new, separate entity, we must use the `copy()` list method invoked on the original `list`. Lists and dictionaries behave this way, but strings and integers do not. Again, there are good reasons for this related to memory management (described in the following subsection), but it can cause a lot of confusion. Variables that hold other variables often behave this way, while variables that hold only raw data often do not. The technical way to describe this behavior is to say that `list` and `dict` variables are mutable (their values can be manipulated in memory), while `str` and `int` variables are immutable (their values cannot be changed after they have been created).

2.14.6 Memory Management with Mutable and Immutable Types

Since `str` variables are immutable, you might wonder what is happening in a line of code such as this:

```
greeting = 'hello' + ' ' + 'world'
greeting
```

'hello world'

Here, three strings are created in memory and then concatenated together. The concatenation is performed in a number of steps equal to the number of strings that are being concatenated minus 1 (2 in this case). First, `'hello'` and `' '` are concatenated. Since strings are immutable, Python cannot change the value of either of the original strings and instead creates a third – `'hello '`. Then, a new string is created from the concatenation of `'hello '` and `'world'` and assigned to the variable `greeting`. This process ends up generating six strings, only one of which is retained (`greeting`). The others stick around in memory until Python disposes of them.

Doing the same thing with a `list` is more memory efficient.

```
greeting = ' '.join(['hello', 'world'])
greeting
```

'hello world'

Here, three strings are created (`'hello'`, `'world'`, and `' '`), as well as the list to hold them. Then, they are joined and assigned to `greeting`; in total, five variables are created instead of six. With small examples like this, the distinction might not seem very important, but as the length of the greeting grows, the number of variables used in the list approach increases linearly while the number used in the string concatenation increases exponentially. With a four-word phrase, the number of variables generated by the list approach is six – one `str` for each word (4); one for the separator character `' '`, one for the `list`; and one for `greeting`. The number generated by the `str` concatenation approach is 14 – one `str` for each word (4); one for each separating space (3); one for each step in the concatenation procedure

(6); and one for greeting. Mutable types like lists and dicts thus provide a significant advantage over str variables for corpus linguists who work with multiple texts that are each many tokens long.

Finally, the mutability of list variables also explains why methods like append() return None instead of a new list. If append() returned a new list, all the values in the list would also have to be copied and assigned to the new list while the old one would just sit in memory until Python had a chance to dispose of it. This would entail significant memory overhead for appending just one value to the list.

2.14.7 Working with Dictionaries

As described in the preceding discussion, dictionaries are like lists in that they hold other variables but differ in that the order of items in a dict cannot be accessed through indexing or slicing. Rather, values (the dictionary equivalent of list elements) are accessed through their keys. Keys are typically strings or integers. There are no type restrictions on values.

Literals in a dict are created using curly braces, { }, and keys are separated from their values using colons :.

```
word_counts = {'beginning': len(words)}
word_counts
```

{'beginning': 8}

We can then access the value associated with a key using square brackets [].

```
word_counts['beginning']
```

8

We can also use a variable to access values as long as the variable is an immutable type.

```
text = 'beginning'
word_counts[text]
```

8

2.14.8 Adding Items to Dictionaries

There is no append() method for dictionaries. To add a new key/value pair, we simply access the dictionary with the new key in square brackets and assign the value to it with the assignment operator =.

```
word_counts['ending'] = len(ending)
word_counts
```

```
{'beginning': 8, 'ending': 7}
```

We now have two items in our dictionary, separated by a comma. Each item is a key and value pair. Changing a value in a dictionary is accomplished in the same way as adding a new value.

```
word_counts['ending'] = 9001
word_counts['ending']
```

```
9001
```

As you might guess, a dictionary's keys must be unique. If we try to add a new value with an existing key, we will simply overwrite the original value for that key.

2.14.9 More on Accessing Items in Dictionaries

We can access a dictionary's keys using the keys() method and its values using the values() method.

```
word_counts.values()
```

```
dict_values([8, 9001])
```

Note that the keys and values are returned as lists (they are in square brackets []). Like all lists, the order of their elements is fixed, and the *i*th key is the key for the *i*th value. This behavior is useful for converting dictionaries to lists. We can also access the items (key/value pairs) independently using the items() dictionary method.

```
word_counts.items()
```

```
dict_items([('beginning', 8), ('ending', 9001)])
```

Here, the return type is a list of tuple variables (each item is enclosed in parentheses). Tuples are a datatype similar to lists, but immutable. We will not be using tuples much in this Element, since in most corpus linguistics tasks that would call for a list-like variable type, it is more efficient to use list, dict, or Series (a column in a dataframe).

2.14.10 Iterating over Lists and Dictionaries

Sometimes, it is desirable to go through every element of a list or dict one at a time. For example, suppose we wanted to test whether each element in a list of tokens is punctuation or a word. To do this, we can use a for loop and the built-in string method isalnum(), which tests whether each character in a string is a letter or number character. If all characters in the string are alphabetical or numeric, the method returns `True`, and if not, `False`.

```
"abcd1359".isalnum()
# returns True because all characters in "abcd1359" are
# either alphabetical or alphanumeric
```

True

```
"?".isalnum()
# returns False because "?" is neither alphabetical nor
# numeric
```

False

```
"abcd123?".isalnum()
# returns False because at least one character in "abcd123?"
# is neither alphabetical nor numeric
```

False

If we want to apply this method to each element in `tokens`, we need to set up a loop to iterate through the elements in `tokens` and invoke the `isalnum()` function on each element.

```
for token in tokens:
    result = token.isalnum()
    print(result)
```

True
True
True
True
True
True
True
False
True
True
True
True
True

```
True
True
```

In the preceding code block, the loop is created using the syntax

`for a in b:`

where b is a list and a is used to refer to the elements in that list. The loop will execute once for each element in b, each time making a refer to the current element. The : indicates that we are beginning a nested block of code. Everything that comes after the : and is indented will be executed on each pass of the loop.

In the preceding case, the code inside the loop executes 15 times (once for each element in tokens). On the first pass through the loop, a refers to the first element of tokens (It). On the second pass, a refers to the second element (was), and so on. Each pass through the loop, the isalnum() method is called on token, and the return value is stored in the variable result. Next, result is printed to the console using the print() function. The upshot of all this is that we end up with a sequence of Trues and Falses printed to the console.

Let us modify the loop so that instead of just printing True or False, we store the result of isalnum() in a list for later use.

```
is_word = []
for token in tokens:
    result = token.isalnum()
    is_word.append(result)

is_word
```

```
[True,
True,
True,
True,
True,
True,
True,
False,
True,
True,
True,
True,
True,
```

```
True,
True]
```

Now, instead of printing to the console, we append each `isalnum()` result to a `list` which we create before the loop begins using

`is_word = []`.

We now have two lists with corresponding indices (`tokens` and `is_word`); since lists are ordered, the *i*th element in `tokens` is associated with the *i*th element in `is_word`. This will be useful later, but we can test that this is the case now. The seventh element in `tokens` should be the punctuation mark . and the corresponding element in `is_word` should be False.

```
tokens[7]
```

`'.'`

```
is_word[7]
```

`False`

2.15 Testing Conditions

One common reason to iterate over a list is to test each element of the list to see whether it meets certain conditions and then execute one set of instructions if it meets those conditions and a different set of conditions if it does not. We can accomplish this with the `if` and `else` keywords.

Let us modify our loop so that as we iterate over `tokens`, we test each element to see whether it is alphanumeric or not. If it is, we will add it to a list of words. If it is not, we will add it to a list of punctuation marks.

```
words = []
punct = []
for token in tokens:
        if token.isalnum():
                words.append(token)
        else:
                punct.append(token)
```

Now we check the values of `words` and `punct` to see if our loop worked.

```
words
```

```
['It',
'was',
'a',
'dark',
'and',
'stormy',
'night',
'and',
'they',
'all',
'lived',
'happily',
'ever',
'after']
```

```
punct
```

```
['.']
```

In the fourth line of our loop, we begin a conditional block using the `if` statement. What follows `if` on the same line is a function that returns either `True` or `False`. As described previously, `isalnum()` returns `True` if all characters in the string are alphanumeric and `False` otherwise, so it works perfectly here. Following the `if` statement is one indented line (the fifth line). This line is executed if `isalnum()` returns `True`. If `isalnum()` returns `False`, however, the indented line after the `else` statement is executed. This creates a fork in the execution of the program. If `isalnum()` returns `True`, the fifth line (but not the seventh) is executed. Elsewise, the seventh line (but not the fifth) is executed.

`if` statements can be followed by functions that return `True` or `False` (called a Boolean variable), but there are other ways to test a condition. For example, the `==` logical operator can be used to test if two variables have the same value (and the same datatype).

```
a == b
```

will evaluate to `True` if a and b are both the string '1', or if both are the integer 1, but not if one is a string '1' and the other is the integer 1.

```
a = '1'
b = '1'

a == b
```

True

```
a = '1'
b = 1

a == b
```

False

We can also test whether a variable equals a literal using the == operator.

```
a = ['hello', 'world']
greeting = ' '.join(a)
greeting == 'hello world'
```

True

```
b = 6 * 4
b == 24
```

True

We can test whether a `list` contains a variable or a literal using the `in` keyword.

```
a = ['hello', 'world']
'world' in a
```

True

```
articles = ['a', 'an', 'the']
for token in tokens:
    if token in articles:
        print(token)
```

a

Finally, following `if` with a variable evaluates to `True` if the variable has a value other than `None`, or `False` if the value of the variable is `None`.

```
a = None
if a:
    print(a)
else:
    print("the variable does not have a value")
```

```
the variable does not have a value
```
With numeric variables, we can use the < (less than), > (greater than), <= (less than or equal to), and >= (greater than or equal to) logical operators to test relative values.

```
a = 5
b = 10

a <= b
```

```
True
```

2.16 Creating Lists and Dictionaries Using Comprehensions

The loop we have worked with is useful, but the syntax is a little clunky. Happily, Python gives us a fast, efficient way of creating lists exactly like the one we just created – the list comprehension. With list comprehensions, we iterate over a list and take elements from that list to create a new one. The basic syntax for a list comprehension is:

```
new_list = [a for a in b]
```
where a is an element of list b. Note that the syntax here combines the syntax for creating a list literal

```
new_list = []
```
with the syntax for iterating over a loop

```
for a in b:
```
There are two notable differences, however. First, there is no : in a list comprehension because there is no nested block of code. List comprehensions are single lines and : is used to indicate the start of a code block. Second, the element that we are taking from list b is included inside the square brackets before the for. We can do any sort of processing of the element we need to before we take it for the new list. For example, we might recreate the functionality of our loop in a list comprehension using

```
is_words = [token.isalnum() for token in tokens]
```

The syntax here says, "Take each element in tokens and apply the isalnum() method to it. Then take the results and store them in a list called is_words."

Dictionary comprehensions can be done in the same way. We combine the syntax for a loop

```
for a in b:
```

with the syntax for creating a `dict` literal

`new_dict = {key: value}`

```
new_dict = {token: token.isalnum() for token in tokens}
new_dict
```

```
{'It': True,
 'was': True,
 'a': True,
 'dark': True,
 'and': True,
 'stormy': True,
 'night': True,
 '.': False,
 'they': True,
 'all': True,
 'lived': True,
 'happily': True,
 'ever': True,
 'after': True}
```

2.17 Iterating over Multiple Variables in One Comprehension

When our data is structured as a table (i.e., in two or more dimensions), it is often desirable to loop through multiple variables; for example, to inspect every cell in a table. To do this, we start by iterating over the rows in a table, but then within each row, iterate over the columns. We can do this by nesting one loop inside of another as in the following code:

First, we will create a table (actually a `list` of `list`s) with three rows and three columns.

```
table = [[1,2,3],
         [4,5,6],
         [7,8,9]]
```

Next, we will iterate over the rows using a `for` loop:

```
for row in table:
    print(row)
```

```
[1, 2, 3]
[4, 5, 6]
[7, 8, 9]
```

We can add a second `for` loop to the first one. When a loop is inside another loop, it is "nested" in the first. When we take all the values from every cell in a table, we are said to be "flattening" it because we have moved the data from a 2-dimensional structure with height and width to a flat, 1-dimensional structure, with width only.

```
for row in table:
    for cell in row:
        print(cell)
```

```
1
2
3
4
5
6
7
8
9
```

We can nest loops in a comprehension with the same comprehension syntax. We just add the second `for` loop.

```
cells = [cell for row in table for cell in row]
print(cells)
```

```
[1, 2, 3, 4, 5, 6, 7, 8, 9]
```

To ease readability, comprehensions with multiple loops can be broken across multiple lines. Comments can be added to help keep things straight.

```
cells = [cell # take the unmodified value of each cell by
    for row in table # iterating over the rows in the table
    for cell in row] # and then each cell in each row
```

List comprehensions provide a fast, memory-efficient way to flatten complicated multidimensional arrays, that is – transform an *n*-dimensional array into a 1-dimensional list.

2.18 Testing Conditions in Comprehensions

Conditions can be included in a list or dictionary comprehension by following the regular syntax with *if*. Multiple conditions can be tested using *and* and *or*.

```
words = [token for token in tokens if token.isalnum()]
words
```

```
['It',
 'was',
 'a',
 'dark',
 'and',
 'stormy',
 'night',
 'and',
 'they',
 'all',
 'lived',
 'happily',
 'ever',
 'after']
```

It is possible to move the conditions after the `if` statement to other lines to keep the list comprehension readable.

```
short_words = [token for token in tokens
               if token.isalnum() and len(token) <= 3]
short_words
```

```
['It', 'was', 'a', 'and', 'and', 'all']
```

2.19 Representing Corpora Using Lists and Dictionaries

At this point, we have much of what we need to start doing CL with Python. Texts can be stored in memory as a list of strings where each string is one token from one text. Additional lists can be used to store metadata so that the *i*th element of each additional list is a piece of metadata about the token at the *i*th position in the first list. We can then pack the lists together into a dictionary where the keys are types of (meta)data, and the values are the lists. We will have created a rudimentary dataframe.

This is where Pandas enters the picture. As noted in Section 1.2, Python does not include datatypes designed specifically for working with data in a tabular structure; hence, the dictionary of rows described previously. Pandas, however, does. In particular, the `DataFrame` datatype provides exactly the table structure shown earlier, but allows us to use a powerful set of methods in the Pandas library to perform common CL tasks. Analysts may learn a relatively small set of methods for counting, sorting, grouping, combining, and modifying rows of a `DataFrame`, and then combine these methods to accomplish a wide range of CL tasks. Section 3 covers these basic building-block methods in detail.

3 Working with DataFrames

This section introduces Pandas `DataFrame` and `Series` classes, methods for loading and saving them to disk, and methods and functions for counting values, grouping rows, and combining values. These form a core set of tools that can be used to accomplish a range of CL tasks. The focus in this section is on explaining these elements generally, while Section 4 describes algorithms that use these procedures to complete CL analyses specifically.

3.1 Pandas DataFrames and Series

We will use two data types extensively in this element, `DataFrames` and `Series`. These are not core data types in Python and must be imported through the Pandas package. However, once imported, we will be able to leverage the powerful methods built into them to do corpus linguistic tasks quickly, reliably, and with minimal hardware resources.

A `Series` is a one-dimensional array of named values – that is, a `list` of values of the same type where each type has an associated name or index. `Series` are very similar to `lists` in that the values they hold are always stored in the same order, but they are more memory efficient and allow vector-based calculations. They are also like dictionaries in that every value in the `Series` has a name or index associated with it. `Series` are useful in part because any element in the `Series` can be accessed with either its name or location.

It may be helpful to think of a `Series` as a column or row in a table or a spreadsheet. A `DataFrame`, by extension, is the whole table or spreadsheet. `Data-Frames` contain one or more `Series` as well as methods for manipulating the entire table.

3.2 Using Pip to Install Pandas and NumPy

Throughout this Element, we will be using `Pandas` for dataframe creation and manipulation. Pandas is a Python package (an add-on that extends Python's functionality). The easiest way to install it is with Pip, Python's built-in package installer. Pip is designed to be run from a command line in Windows. To access the command line, press the Windows Key + r and then type cmd. This will bring up a command-line interface. If your Python path has been added to the system path, you can now install any Python package simply by typing `pip install` and the name of the package.

```
pip install pandas
```

installs Pandas. Be careful with the names of packages; they are case sensitive.

This installation process will automatically install other packages that Pandas requires. One of these is NumPy, a package that contains functions and data-types for an array of efficient mathematical operations. If, for some reason, NumPy is not automatically installed with Pandas, you can install it with

```
pip install numpy
```

All code in this Element will run with Pandas version 2.0 or higher and NumPy 1.24 or higher. Pip will install the most recent versions of packages available for your current version of Python, however, so it should not be necessary to manage versions manually.

3.3 Loading and Inspecting a Pandas `DataFrame` Corpus

The following code instructs Python to make all the datatypes and functions in the Pandas library available to the user and then reads a `DataFrame` corpus into memory (assuming the CORE.pickle file is in your current working directory). Note that the `DataFrame` version of CORE is stored on disk in Python's `pickle` format – a compact, though not compressed, file type.

```
import pandas as pd
c = pd.read_pickle('CORE.pickle')
```

Here, the corpus is read from a file into memory as a `DataFrame` and given the name `c`. Throughout this Element, `c` is used as a variable name for dataframe corpora. It is not necessary to be so terse. Indeed, it is more in keeping with the spirit of Python to name it something like `corpus`, `CORE_corpus`, or `CORE_dataframe`, but keep in mind that you will be typing the name of this variable often.

We can see the dimensions of the `DataFrame` (the number of rows and columns) using the `shape` property.

```
c.shape # returns the shape of the DataFrame (rows, columns)
```

```
(69933607, 7)
```

The value here is a `tuple` with two elements. The first indicates that there are 69,933,607 rows in this `DataFrame`. The second indicates that there are seven columns. If we want to know only the number of rows, we can access only the first element. Likewise, the second element tells us the number of columns. We can access the number of columns or rows through list indexing with square brackets (remember that lists are zero-based in Python).

```
c.shape[0] # returns the number of rows
```

```
69933607
```

```
c.shape[1] # returns the number of columns
```

```
7
```

To view the first *n* lines of the dataframe, we can use the method `head(n)` invoked on the `DataFrame`. We can view the last *n* lines with `tail(n)`. We see the head and tail together (with the body elided) if we just call or print `print()` the name of the DataFrame.

```
c.head(3)
```

	token	type	lemma	tag	pos	text	register
0	I	i	I	PRP	PRON	1465224	av
1	'm	am	be	VBP	AUX	1465224	av
2	22	22	22	CD	NUM	1465224	av

```
c.tail(3)
```

	token	type	lemma	tag	pos	text	register
69933604	.	.	.	.	PUNCT	0344188	tv
69933605	hide	hide	hide	VB	VERB	0344188	tv
69933606	link	link	link	NN	NOUN	0344188	tv

```
c
```

	token	type	lemma	tag	pos	text	register
0	I	i	I	PRP	PRON	1465224	av
1	'm	am	be	VBP	AUX	1465224	av
2	22	22	22	CD	NUM	1465224	av
3	and	and	and	CC	CCONJ	1465224	av
4	I	i	I	PRP	PRON	1465224	av
...	...	...	...	...	...	...	...
69933602	or	or	or	CC	CCONJ	0344188	tv
69933603	webpage	webpage	webpage	NN	NOUN	0344188	tv
69933604	.	.	.	.	PUNCT	0344188	tv
69933605	hide	hide	hide	VB	VERB	0344188	tv
69933606	link	link	link	NN	NOUN	0344188	tv

```
[69933607 rows x 7 columns]
```

Here we see the basic structure of our dataframe corpus. The `DataFrame` has an index column, which contains numeric indices for each row in the

DataFrame. The index starts at 0 for the first row and runs all the way to 69,933,606 for the last. The numeric value of the index for the ith row is thus i-1.

As described earlier, the columns (not including the index) are labeled token, type, lemma, tag, pos, text, and register. Refer to the description of the corpus in Section 1.4 for more information.

Each of these columns is a Pandas Series, which we can access using the . operator after the name of DataFrame. The . operator is used to access the methods and properties of a variable. Columns in Pandas DataFrames are properties with the Series datatype.

```
c.token.head(3)
```

```
0    I
1    'm
2    22
```

```
Name: token, dtype: category
Categories (514936, object): [' ', '', '!', '"', ..., 'vouchsaf-
ing', 'wizzle', 'www.safetourist.org', 'www.wilderness']
```

It is also possible to access a column using Python's dictionary lookup notation.

```
c['tag'].head(3)
```

```
0    PRP
1    VBP
2    CD
```

```
Name: tag, dtype: category
Categories (49, object): ['$', '''', ',', '-LRB-', ..., 'WP$',
'WRB', 'XX', '``']
```

Using the dictionary lookup notation, but not the . operator, we can access multiple columns by passing a list of column names into the square brackets [] (note that the set of square brackets defining the list literal must be included in addition to the set of square brackets used to access the DataFrame's dictionary of columns).

```
c[['type', 'tag']].head(3)
```

```
       type      tag
0      i         PRP
1      am        VBP
2      22        CD
```

When we access a single column, Python displays its head and tail with the body replaced with ellipses as well as a bit of extra information at the bottom: the name of the column, the length (number of elements), and the column's datatype (columns cannot contain data of multiple types).

```
c.tag
```

```
0               PRP
1               VBP
2               CD
3               CC
4               PRP
                ...
69933602        CC
69933603        NN
69933604        .
69933605        VB
69933606        NN
```

```
Name: tag, Length: 69933607, dtype: category
Categories (49, object): ['$', '''', ',', '-LRB-', ..., 'WP$',
'WRB', 'XX', '``']
```

You may expect that the datatype for all our columns would be `string`, but as indicated earlier, the datatype is actually `category`. Therefore, we also see the number of categories and a partial list of all the categories in the column.

3.4 The Category Datatype

The `category` datatype is essential for making `DataFrame` corpora easy to manipulate. It does this by reducing the amount of memory required by the `DataFrame`. Imagine a dataframe with a million rows and five columns where every cell contains a `string` variable. Storing this dataframe in memory would require Python to manage five million strings. The amount of memory used for one string varies, but 55 bytes per string is a reasonable estimate for lengths we are likely to encounter. Five million strings at 55 bytes per string works out to 275 megabytes of memory. For a one-million-word corpus, this is not prohibitive for most modern computers, but a 100-million-word corpus like the British National Corpus would require 27.5 gigabytes of memory just to store the elements in the cells of the dataframe.

The `category` datatype reduces the amount of memory needed by creating a dictionary of values in the column and mapping them to integer keys. This allows integers to be stored in the dataframe instead of strings. As integers require less memory, the full column takes up less space. This also increases performance on operations like sorting and searching because the algorithms operate on a smaller memory space. What is more, the increased memory and performance efficiency of categories over strings increases as the ratio of the number of unique values in a column to the total number of values in the column decreases. This means columns with a small number of often-repeated values (e.g., part-of-speech tags, file names) will benefit more by being stored as categories than columns with a greater number of unique values repeated less frequently (e.g., tokens, types), but any column with repeated values will take less memory as `category` than as `string`.

3.5 Creating DataFrames

`DataFrames` can be created by passing data into Pandas' `DataFrame()` function. The `DataFrame()` function can accept data in a range of different formats, but the most straightforward approach is to pass it in a dictionary where the keys are `strings` with the names of columns and the values are `lists` containing the values for that column. Typically, this is done using the syntax

```
df = pd.DataFrame({'a': a,
                   'b': b})
```

where a and b are lists of the same length. Consider the following code.

```
df = pd.DataFrame({'col1': ['a', 'b', 'c'],
                   'col2': [1, 2, 3]})
df
```

```
    col1    col2
0    a       1
1    b       2
2    c       3
```

A `DataFrame`'s column names can be accessed with the `columns` property, which can also be used to rename its columns.

```
df.columns
```

```
Index(['col1', 'col2'], dtype='object')
```

```
df.columns = ['letters', 'numbers']
df
```

```
   letters  numbers
0  a        1
1  b        2
2  c        3
```

Columns can be inserted into a `DataFrame` with `insert()` where the first argument is the index of the inserted column, the second is the name of the column, and the third is a list of column values.

```
df.insert(0, 'symbols', ['!', '@', '#'])
df
```

```
   symbols  letters  numbers
0  !        a        1
1  @        b        2
2  #        c        3
```

It is also possible to create a `DataFrame` by passing a list of `list` or `Series` for the rows and a list of `strings` or `integers` as column names using `columns=`. Consider the following code:

```
s1 = ['!', 'a', 1]
s2 = ['@', 'b', 2]
s3 = ['#', 'c', 3]
rows = [s1, s2, s3]
names = ['symbols', 'letters', 'numbers']

df = pd.DataFrame(rows, columns=names)
df
```

```
   symbols  letters  numbers
0  !        a        1
1  @        b        2
2  #        c        3
```

The two approaches produce equivalent `DataFrames`, but the first is useful if the raw data are stored as columns and the second if they come in rows. You may be curious as to how to take text data from files and transform them into columns or rows – that is, how to create a dataframe corpus from text files. An algorithm for doing so is presented in Section 5. You may also be interested in how to save a dataframe corpus that you have created or modified to disk. This is covered in Section 3.6.2.

3.6 Core Methods

3.6.1 Counting Values – Frequency and Normalized Frequency

Many common corpus linguistic tasks require counting the number of times a word occurs in a corpus. With `DataFrame` corpora, this may be done by invoking the `value_counts()` method on the column of the `DataFrame` we wish to count in.

```
counts = c.type.value_counts()
counts.head()
```

```
type

the   3353004
.     2744928
,     2732675
to    1746985
and   1646234
```

```
Name: count, dtype: int64
```

Here, the `type` column is accessed using `c.type` and then the values in it are counted using `value_counts()`. The `value_counts()` method returns a sorted `Series`, which we then assign to the variable `counts`. Note here that the index of this `Series` is not numerical (as the index of `c` is). Rather, the index contains all the categories from the `type` column. Another way to think of this is that the numbers produced by the `value_counts()` method are indexed by their category (in this case, the word type) rather than by a location in the corpus (which would not make sense). We can access the frequency for a specific word in the same way we would look up a value in a dictionary with a key.

```
counts['order']
```

```
19744
```

Here, we use square brackets to look up the frequency of *order* in `counts` and find that it occurs 19,744 times.

We may wish to normalize these counts to a standard number of words to facilitate cross-corpus comparisons. To do this, we pass into the `value_counts()` method the `normalize=True` argument and multiply by the integer we wish to normalize to.

```
normed_counts = c.type.value_counts(normalize=True) * 100
normed_counts.head()
```

```
type

the     4.794553
.       3.925049
,       3.907528
to      2.498062
and     2.353996
```

Name: proportion, dtype: float64

Now we see that *the* occurs about 4.8 times per hundred words. The normalized frequency of any word type in the corpus can be found by looking up the word in the `Series` index.

```
normed_counts['order']
```

0.028232491997731507

Without realizing it, we have leveraged one of Pandas greatest advantages – the ability to do vector-based calculations. Here, we multiply a `Series` by a single value. Pandas automatically knows to multiply each element in the `Series` by 100 and return a `Series` of the same length as the original with the same index. Because Pandas' vector-based operations are implemented with highly optimized code, they are extremely fast to execute. Vector-based multiplication with `normed_counts` takes less than a millisecond, while alternate approaches may take orders of magnitude longer.

Whenever speed is an issue, we should use vector-based calculations. Pandas can perform basic arithmetic operations (+, -, /, and *) as well as the modular division operator (%) and the equivalence test operator (==) this way. A wider range of mathematical operations can be applied to `Series` using functions in the NumPy package.

3.6.2 Exporting DataFrames and Series to Files or the Clipboard

`normed_counts` contains information about the frequency of word types in our corpus, but viewing the series on the console only displays its head and tail. The series is also lost when the script ends, or when the application we used to run the code closes. Accordingly, we will often wish to export `DataFrames` to files for later use. We can do this using the `to_csv()` method.

The csv (comma separated values) file format stores tabular data as plain text. When a table is stored as .csv, each column is delimited with a comma (or tab), and each row is delimited with a return character. All the data in the cells of a .csv file are stored as plain text.

The `to_csv()` method takes a string as its first argument – the path for the . csv file. In Windows, passing "data.csv" into `to_csv()` creates a file called data.csv in the current working directory (or overwrites it if the file already exists).

If you are exporting a `DataFrame`, you may add a header row with the names of columns to the .csv file by including the argument `header=True` after the string with the file path. If you are exporting a `Series`, however, you may want to pass `header=False` as the second argument.

Finally, since many tokens may be commas, we should use the tab whitespace character as the separator character. We can indicate this with the `sep='\t'` argument (note that \t refers to the white space indentation that is created when the tab key is pressed in a text editor or word processor).

To export our `normed_counts Series` to a file, we use

```
normed_counts.to_csv(path, header=False, sep='\t')
```

where *path* is a string with the location at which we wish to save the file.

Exporting a `DataFrame` to a file is not always necessary. At times, you may want to export your data to the system clipboard so it can be pasted into spreadsheet software, or imported to another programming language as a dataframe. To do this, use the `to_clipboard()` method. This method does not require a file path, but by default still formats the data on the clipboard as a .csv file. Therefore, the `header=True` or `header=False` and `sep='\t'` arguments are still necessary. Alternately, you may wish to export the file to the clipboard in Excel format. In this case, the argument `excel=True` should be included and the `header` and `sep` arguments omitted.

```
normed_counts.to_clipboard(header=False, sep='\t')
```

or

```
normed_counts.to_clipboard(excel=True)
```

3.6.3 Measuring Range

We may wish to find the number or proportion of texts that a word occurs in (its range), or we may wish to find the frequency of every word in every text in which it appears. Both can be accomplished with Pandas' `groupby()` method. `groupby()` takes all the rows in a `DataFrame` and groups them together with other rows that share a value in one or more columns. We can then apply one of a limited range of methods to each group. These methods summarize relevant characteristics of the group. This is useful if we wish to treat word types or texts as units of analysis.

```
ranges = c.groupby('type').text.nunique()
ranges = ranges.sort_values(ascending=False)
ranges.head()
```

```
type

the    48493
.      48290
,      48261
and    48238
to     48229

Name: text, dtype: int64
```

Here, we group the rows of the corpus by word type, access the text column of each group, and then count the number of unique values that occur in the text column for each group using `nunique()`. Since each group is a word type, the resulting `Series` lists the ranges for every type in the corpus. Then, we sort the `Series` using `sort_values()`. By default, this method returns a `Series` sorted in ascending order. However, we can tell Pandas to sort in descending order with the argument `ascending=False`. Finally, we assign this series to the variable `ranges` and display its head on the console.

The results indicate that *the* is the type with the greatest range (it occurs in 48,493 texts), while . occurs in 48,290. It may be more useful to know the proportion of texts that each word occurs in. We can learn this by dividing the range for each type by the total number of texts in the corpus – a number we can get by accessing the text column of the `DataFrame` and invoking the `nunique()` method.

```
n_texts = c.text.nunique()
ranges_prop = ranges / n_texts
ranges_prop.head()
```

```
type
```

```
the      0.998394
.        0.994215
,        0.993618
and      0.993144
to       0.992959
```

```
Name: text, dtype: float64
```

3.6.4 Indexing and Filtering

So far, we have been operating on entire columns of a dataframe, but many CL tasks require looking only at specific words or words within a predefined set. With Pandas, there are a variety of ways to zero in on specific rows. The most straightforward of these is to index a `DataFrame` or `Series` using square brackets []. As with `lists`, the elements of a `Series` can be accessed by their indices as one might do with a `dict`. In what follows, we get the frequencies and ranges we have calculated thus far for the word type *misinformation*.

```
counts['misinformation']
```

262

```
normed_counts['misinformation']
```

0.0003746410506181956

```
ranges['misinformation']
```

192

This approach works because we have already created the `Series` with the appropriate counts. However, a more flexible way to learn about specific words is to use Pandas' ability to select lines from a `DataFrame` that meet certain conditions and return only those lines as a new `DataFrame`. This is done using the `loc` property of `DataFrames` or `Series` with methods like `eq()` which returns `True` for every value in a `Series` that is equal to a value (`eq()` is identical to the equivalence test operator `==` used in the previous section). For example, we can find all rows in our corpus where the word type is *misinformation* using

```
rows = c.loc[c.type.eq('misinformation')]
rows.head()
```

```
        token            type             lemma           tag  pos   text \
434241  misinformation   misinformation   misinformation  NN   NOUN  3243290
842744  misinformation   misinformation   misinformation  NN   NOUN  0453603
966462  misinformation   misinformation   misinformation  NN   NOUN  0413412
976671  misinformation   misinformation   misinformation  NN   NOUN  3115141
976811  misinformation   misinformation   misinformation  NN   NOUN  3115141


        register
434241          av
842744          av
966462          av
976671          av
976811          av
```

loc is an indexer. It is not a method, but rather a property that works a lot like
a Python dictionary. Just as we can look up a value in a dict by passing in
a key, we can use loc to look up a row (the value) with the label of that row in
the index (the key). The syntax for doing this is identical to the syntax for
looking up a value in a dictionary.

c.loc[500]

will return the row (as a Series) with the label 500 in the index of the
DataFrame.

```
c.loc[500]
```

```
token     do
type      do
lemma     do
tag       VBP
pos       AUX
text      1465224
register  av
```

Name: 500, dtype: object

Unlike dictionaries, however, the loc indexer is very flexible in the type of data
that can be used to look up values. For one, we can look up a set of sequential
rows in the DataFrame using the slice notation for lists – the lower bound,
followed by a colon :, followed by the upper bound.

```
c.loc[500:505]
```

Corpus Linguistics

	token	type	lemma	tag	pos	text	register
500	do	do	do	VBP	AUX	1465224	av
501	n't	not	not	RB	PART	1465224	av
502	have	have	have	VB	AUX	1465224	av
503	to	to	to	TO	PART	1465224	av
504	get	get	get	VB	VERB	1465224	av
505	drunk	drunk	drunk	JJ	ADJ	1465224	av

Note here that the behavior of `loc` with a slice differs slightly from the behavior of lists. The upper bound (505 in the preceding code sample) is included in the slice returned by `loc`, but would not be included in the same slice of a list. We can test this by taking a column of the `DataFrame`, converting it to a list, and slicing it.

```
c.type.tolist()[500:505]
```

['do', 'not', 'have', 'to', 'get']

The final row with the token *drunk* in the slice returned by `loc` is not included in the list slice.

In addition to single values and slices, it is also possible to give `loc` a `list` of row labels. The `loc` indexer will return a `DataFrame` with one row for each value in the set or list.

```
indices = [0, 5, 15, 20]
c.loc[indices]
```

	token	type	lemma	tag	pos	text	register
0	I	i	I	PRP	PRON	1465224	av
5	've	have	've	VBP	AUX	1465224	av
15	so	so	so	RB	ADV	1465224	av
20	mind	mind	mind	VB	VERB	1465224	av

Finally, we can give `loc` a `list` or `Series` of True / False values of the same length as the number of rows in the `DataFrame` and `loc` will return all the rows that correspond to a `True` value.

```
# create a mini-corpus with just the five rows of the corpus
# DataFrame
mini_corpus = c[:5]
# create a list with five True / False values.
indices = [False, True, False, False, True]
# loc the indices that correspond to True in the indices list
mini_corpus.loc[indices]
```

	token	type	lemma	tag	pos	text	register
1	'm	am	be	VBP	AUX	1465224	av
4	I	i	I	PRP	PRON	1465224	av

This last approach to using `loc` is the key to locating rows that meet certain conditions. Because we can very easily get `Series` of True / False values using the `eq()` method, we can quickly locate all rows that meet the condition. Now we can see why

```
c.loc[c.type.eq('misinformation')]
```

finds all the rows of the `DataFrame` where the value of the `type` column is *misinformation*:

```
c.type.eq('misinformation')
```

returns a `Series` of `True` or `False` values and `c.loc[]` returns all the rows that correspond to `True` in that `Series`.

It is possible to use this approach to apply multiple conditions. If we want to extract only those rows where the `type` column is equal to *misinformation* and the `register` column is equal to *ne* (news), we can do so by including multiple logical tests inside the square brackets `[]` after `loc`.

```
rows = c.loc[c.type.eq('misinformation') & c.register.eq
('ne')]
rows.head()
```

	token	type	lemma	tag	pos	text \
26383062	misinformation	misinformation	misinformation	NN	NOUN	0094414
26533219	misinformation	misinformation	misinformation	NN	NOUN	0098047
26606785	misinformation	misinformation	misinformation	NN	NOUN	0471982
26633396	misinformation	misinformation	misinformation	NN	NOUN	0589360
26852843	misinformation	misinformation	misinformation	NN	NOUN	0403213

	register
26383062	ne
26533219	ne
26606785	ne
26633396	ne
26852843	ne

Each condition must be joined with & to indicate *and*, or | to indicate *or*. A ~ can be placed in front of a condition to mean *not*. The following code locates instances of *misinformation* from registers other than news.

```
rows = c.loc[c.type.eq('misinformation') &
~c.register.eq('ne')]
rows.head()
```

```
         token              type              lemma        tag pos  text \
434241 misinformation misinformation misinformation NN  NOUN 3243290
842744 misinformation misinformation misinformation NN  NOUN 0453603
966462 misinformation misinformation misinformation NN  NOUN 0413412
976671 misinformation misinformation misinformation NN  NOUN 3115141
976811 misinformation misinformation misinformation NN  NOUN 3115141

            register
434241         av
842744         av
966462         av
976671         av
976811         av
```

3.6.5 Selecting Rows before or after Rows that Meet a Condition and Removing Unused Categories

Often, we may search for a word not because we are interested in the word itself, but rather what comes before or after it. We can do this by rolling the dataframe forward or backward using

```
shift(n)
```

where *n* is an integer. shift(n) moves the content of the DataFrame forward n rows such that row *i* becomes row *i* + *n*. Consider the examples below.

```
c.head()
```

```
   token type lemma tag  pos    text    register
0  I     i    I     PRP  PRON   1465224 av
1  'm    am   be    VBP  AUX    1465224 av
2  22    22   22    CD   NUM    1465224 av
3  and   and  and   CC   CCONJ  1465224 av
4  I     i    I     PRP  PRON   1465224 av
```

```
c.shift(1).head()
```

	token	type	lemma	tag	pos	text	register
0	NaN	NaN	NaN	NaN	NaN	NaN	NaN
1	I	i	I	PRP	PRON	1465224	av
2	'm	am	be	VBP	AUX	1465224	av
3	22	22	22	CD	NUM	1465224	av
4	and	and	and	CC	CCONJ	1465224	av

After shifting the dataframe forward 1 row, row 0 becomes row 1, 1 becomes 2, 2 becomes 3, and so on. Row 0 is populated with null values (NaN). DataFrames can also be shifted backward by passing a negative integer into shift(). This makes row 1 become 0, 2 become 1, 3 become 2, and so on.

```
c.shift(-1).head()
```

	token	type	lemma	tag	pos	text	register
0	'm	am	be	VBP	AUX	1465224	av
1	22	22	22	CD	NUM	1465224	av
2	and	and	and	CC	CCONJ	1465224	av
3	I	i	I	PRP	PRON	1465224	av
4	've	have	've	VBP	AUX	1465224	av

This allows us to locate rows that come after or before rows that meet certain conditions. If we are interested in finding the set of words that come immediately after personal pronouns, we need only shift the DataFrame forward one row and find all rows with a personal pronoun tag (PRP) in the tag column.

```
df = c.loc[c.shift(1).tag.eq('PRP')]
df.head()
```

	token	type	lemma	tag	pos	text	register
1	'm	am	be	VBP	AUX	1465224	av
5	've	have	've	VBP	AUX	1465224	av
18	did	do	do	VBD	AUX	1465224	av
44	'm	am	be	VBP	AUX	1465224	av
61	left	left	leave	VBD	VERB	1465224	av

We can then get frequency counts for these words using value_counts().

```
df.type.value_counts().head()
```

```
type
```

```
ve       195496
have     160875
are      146721
was      133186
's       122563
Name: count, dtype: int64
```

If you inspect the end of the Series using `tail()`, you may notice that many of the counts produced by `value_counts()` are 0.

```
df.type.value_counts().tail()
```

```
type
```

```
enda            0
emmettleffel    0
emedica         0
embaressing     0
zicha           0
```

```
Name: count, dtype: int64
```

These word types never occur in rows immediately before rows with personal pronouns. They are included in the output because when `value_counts()` is invoked on a column of the `category` datatype, the method produces counts for all categories in the column even if the value is 0. To drop these excess categories, we can invoke the `cat.remove_unused_categories()` method of the `type` column before we invoke `value_counts()`.

```
df2 = df.type.cat.remove_unused_categories()
df2.value_counts().tail()
```

```
type
```

```
disarmed        1
disgraceful     1
dispelled       1
disperses       1
hippopotamic    1
Name: count, dtype: int64
```

In the preceding code we chain together several Pandas methods. First, we access the `type` column. Then we remove unused categories using `cat.`

`remove_unused_categories()`. Then we count the remaining values using `value_counts()`. Finally, we display the tail of the `dataframe` using `tail ()`. This is a natural way to manipulate Pandas `DataFrames`, but occasionally, the resulting code gets too long to be readable. In these cases, it is possible to break the command across several lines by enclosing it in parentheses () and indenting one level.

```
(
    df.type
    .cat.remove_unused_categories()
    .value_counts()
    .tail()
)
```

```
type

disarmed      1
disgraceful   1
dispelled     1
disperses     1
hippopotamic  1
```

`Name: count, dtype: int64`
We may also use Python's line continuation character \ between the chained methods to split a long sequence of methods across multiple lines.

```
df.type.cat.remove_unused_categories().\
value_counts().tail()
```

```
type

disarmed      1
disgraceful   1
dispelled     1
disperses     1
hippopotamic  1
```

`Name: count, dtype: int64`

3.6.6 Finding Words Using Wildcards and Regular Expressions

You may wish to filter a `DataFrame` for tokens that start or end with a certain letter sequence or that contain a certain substring. Pandas provides support for these tasks through the `str` module, which can be invoked through the .

operator after the name of a column. In particular, three methods are useful here: `str.beginswith()`, `str.endswith()`, and `str.contains()`. The following code, for example, selects only those rows with values in the `type` column that begin with "un".

```
un = c.loc[c.type.str.startswith('un')]
un.head()
```

	token	type	lemma	tag	pos	text	register
138	unachievable	unachievable	unachievable	JJ	ADJ	1465224	av
381	unachievable	unachievable	unachievable	JJ	ADJ	1465224	av
391	unless	unless	unless	IN	SCONJ	1465224	av
1097	under	under	under	IN	ADP	3037012	av
1823	Unwittingly	unwittingly	unwittingly	RB	ADV	0290769	av

Similarly, we might select rows with values in the `type` column that end with "-ing" and with values in the `tag` column that are verb tags.

```
ing_verbs = c.loc[(c.type.str.endswith('ing')) &
(c.tag.str.startswith('V'))]
ing_verbs.head()
```

	token	type	lemma	tag	pos	text	register
22	having	having	have	VBG	VERB	1465224	av
37	going	going	go	VBG	VERB	1465224	av
107	having	having	have	VBG	VERB	1465224	av
122	going	going	go	VBG	VERB	1465224	av
128	looking	looking	look	VBG	VERB	1465224	av

In these examples, we passed `strings` into Pandas str methods (`str.startswith()`, `str.endswith()`). It is also possible to search for values that match a regular expression pattern using `str.contains()`, as you can see in the next example.

```
c.loc[c.type.str.contains('^un.+ing$')]
```

	token	type	lemma	tag	pos	text \
6793	understanding	understanding	understanding	NN	NOUN	0680482
6806	underlying	underlying	underlying	JJ	ADJ	0680482
10250	understanding	understanding	understand	VBG	VERB	1804331
20960	understanding	understanding	understand	VBG	VERB	0208520
32912	understanding	understanding	understanding	NN	NOUN	0245302

69847836	undergoing	undergoing	undergo	VBG	VERB	0787810
69863913	unenlightening	unenlightening	unenlightene	VBG	VERB	0758536
69872589	undulating	undulating	undulate	VBG	VERB	0425080
69899180	understanding	understanding	understanding	NN	NOUN	0471174
69905544	unknowing	unknowing	unknowing	JJ	ADJ	0532948

	register
6793	av
6806	av
10250	av
20960	av
32912	av
...	...
69847836	tb
69863913	tb
69872589	tb
69899180	tv
69905544	tv

[15076 rows x 7 columns]

The string

`'^un.+ing$'`

is a regular expression pattern indicating the sequence *un* at the start of a string (^un), followed by one or more occurrences of any character (.+), followed by the sequence *ing* at the end of the string (ing$). The results include the range of words that fit this pattern.

A full treatment of regular expressions is outside the scope of this Element, but it is worth noting here that the behavior of Pandas' string methods may not match expectations if your search term includes characters that have special meaning in a regular expression. For example, the ^, ., +, and $ characters in the preceding string are recognized as special characters. Respectively, they match the beginning of a string, any character, any number of repetitions from one to infinity, and the end of a string. Searching for them may produce unexpected results. If we want to find any type that includes a ".", for example, we might be surprised if we use

`str.contains('.')`

```
c.loc[c.type.str.contains('.')].head()
```

	token	type	lemma	tag	pos	text	register
0	I	i	I	PRP	PRON	1465224	av
1	'm	am	be	VBP	AUX	1465224	av
2	22	22	22	CD	NUM	1465224	av
3	and	and	and	CC	CCONJ	1465224	av
4	I	i	I	PRP	PRON	1465224	av

Because the . character is used by the regular expression engine to match any character, Pandas matches every row that contains any character (i.e., all of them). To search for just rows where the type column contains a string with a . in it, we need to tell Pandas to treat the string argument for `str.contains()` as a `string` literal, not a regular expression pattern. We do this by passing in another argument, `regex=False`.

```
c.loc[c.type.str.contains('.', regex=False)].head()
```

	token	type	lemma	tag	pos	text	register
10	..	..	..	NFP	PUNCT	1465224	av
11	.	.	.	.	PUNCT	1465224	av
59	.	.	.	.	PUNCT	1465224	av
78	.	.	.	.	PUNCT	1465224	av
101	.	.	.	.	PUNCT	1465224	av

3.6.7 Finding Any Word in a List

Suppose you want to search for any one of a set of words. For example, we may be interested in contrasting verbs with similar meanings, but different argument structures such as *fill*, *pour*, and *load*. We can instruct Pandas to filter the DataFrame for these words using the `isin()` method with a `list` of values to search for as the argument.

```
lemmas = ['fill', 'pour', 'load']
c.loc[(c.lemma.isin(lemmas)) &
        (c.tag.str.startswith('V'))].head()
```

	token	type	lemma	tag	pos	text	register
7377	fill	fill	fill	VB	VERB	0680482	av
65079	filled	filled	fill	VBN	VERB	3084729	av
65439	Fill	fill	fill	VB	VERB	3084729	av
79585	Fill	fill	fill	VB	VERB	3252069	av
88763	load	load	load	VBP	VERB	3311654	av

3.6.8 Finding Multiword Strings

It is possible to search for sequences of values using shift(). We previously used shift() to find rows that came before or after rows that met certain conditions. We can also use shift() to apply conditions to multiple rows. In this way we can test whether the type in row *n* is the first word of a multiword sequence, the type in row *n*+1 is the second word in a multiword sequence, and so on. If, for example, we want to look for the string *i used to*, we can search using the following conditions:

```
c.type.eq('i')
c.shift(-1).type.eq('used')
c.shift(-2).type.eq('to')
```

This will identify rows where the type column equals *i*, the type column in the next row equals *used*, and the type column in the row after that equals *to*.

```
rows = c.loc[c.type.eq('i') &
  c.shift(-1).type.eq('used') &
  c.shift(-2).type.eq('to')]
rows.head()
```

	token	type	lemma	tag	pos	text	register
21833	I	i	I	PRP	PRON	0522112	av
21901	I	i	I	PRP	PRON	0522112	av
22752	I	i	I	PRP	PRON	0522112	av
44021	I	i	I	PRP	PRON	0564626	av
105647	I	i	I	PRP	PRON	0120208	av

Python finds several instances of the sequence *i used to*, but returns only the first row in each sequence. This is because the unshifted value in our search term is the first word in the sequence. We can get a sense of the wider linguistic context for these sequences by constructing a context window for each hit (context windows are discussed in the next section), but there are times when we are interested instead in the possible values of a variable slot in a multiword sequence. If we are interested in learning, for example, which words can fill the * position in the lexical bundle *on the * hand*, we can search for rows with *on* in the type column two rows before (using shift(2)), *the* one row before (using shift(1)), and *hand* one row after (using shift(-1)).

```
df = c.loc[c.shift(2).type.eq('on') &
          c.shift(1).type.eq('the') &
          c.shift(-1).type.eq('hand')]
(
```

```
    df.type.
    cat.remove_unused_categories().
    value_counts()
    )
```

```
type

other       2724
one          429
right         58
left          44
2nd            1
engine         1
first          1
same           1
wrong          1
invisible      1
```

Name: count, dtype: int64

Here, we did not set a condition on the unshifted row, so it is not referred to in the square brackets after `loc` – we want to retrieve *all* rows that come after *on the* and before *hand*. Python returns the `DataFrame` with those rows and we store it in `df`. Then we access the `type` column, remove unused categories, and count the values that are left.

The results indicate that *on the other hand* is mostly fixed in this corpus. The overwhelming majority of instances of *on the * hand* occurs with either *other* or *one* in the * position.

3.7 Working with Larger Units: *N*-grams and Context Windows

3.7.1 Constructing N-grams

Linguists interested in finding sequences of tokens may use Pandas methods to convert a dataframe corpus to *n*-grams, *n*-length sequences of tokens. This may be done using the `cat()` method in Pandas' `Series.str` module. When invoked on a column of a dataframe, `str.cat()` returns the values of the column concatenated into a single string. The `others=` argument, however, can be used to concatenate the values of two columns together where each value is the concatenation of the values in the same row of the two columns. The `sep=` argument tells Pandas which character to place between the concatenated values. For example, we can use str.cat() to concatenate every word type with the part of speech tag in the same row.

```
type_tag_pairs = c.type.str.cat(others=c.tag, sep='_')
type_tag_pairs.head()
```

```
0       i_PRP
1       am_VBP
2       22_CD
3       and_CC
4       i_PRP
```

Name: type, dtype: object

With shift(), however, str.cat() can be used to concatenate sequential values in the same column.

`c.type.str.cat(others=c.type.shift(-1), sep=" ")`

concatenates each value in the type column with each value in the same row when c.type is shifted one rank backward. In other words, it concatenates each value in the type column with the value in the subsequent row. The sep= " " argument tells Pandas to place a whitespace character between each of the values that are concatenated together. As there is no next row for the last row in the DataFrame, the value in that slot is null (NaN).

```
c.type.str.cat(others=c.type.shift(-1), sep=" ").head()
```

```
0   i       am
1   am      22
2   22      and
3   and     i
4   i       have
```
Name: type, dtype: object

The others= argument usually takes a single Series, but if we pass into the method a list of Series, it will concatenate values from each. For example,

`c.token.str.cat(others=[c.type, c.lemma, c.tag], sep=" ")`

concatenates the value in the token column of each row with the values in the type, lemma, and tag columns of the same row.

```
c.token.str.cat(others=[c.type, c.lemma, c.tag],
sep="_").head()
```

```
0       I_i_I_PRP
1       'm_am_be_VBP
2       22_22_22_CD
3   and_and_and_CC
4       I_i_I_PRP
```
Name: token, dtype: object

We can use this procedure to concatenate multiple sequential values by passing in a list with multiple shifts of the same column.

```
c.type.str.cat(others=[c.type.shift(-1),
                       c.type.shift(-2),
                       c.type.shift(-3)],
               sep=" ").head()
```

```
0    i am 22 and
1    am 22 and i
2    22 and i have
3    and i have never
4    i have never had
Name: type, dtype: object
```

In the preceding example, we concatenate each value in the type column with the values in the type column one, two, and three rows after it. Thus, the list we passed with others= was

`[c.type.shift(-1), c.type.shift(-2), c.type.shift(-3)]`

Manually creating a list of values to concatenate is fine, but tedious for longer sequences. We can create a compact list of values to concatenate using a list comprehension of the form

`[c.type.shift(-i) for i in range(1, n)]`

where n is the number of words we wish to include in the *n*-gram. The following code creates a list of three-grams.

```
n=3
shifted_cols = [c.type.shift(-i) for i in range(1, n)]
ngrams = c.type.str.cat(others=shifted_cols, sep=" ")
ngrams.head()
```

```
0    i am 22
1    am 22 and
2    22 and i
3    and i have
4    i have never
Name: type, dtype: object
```

To create a list of four-grams, we need only change the value of n from 3 to 4.

```
n=4
shifted_cols = [c.type.shift(-i) for i in range(1, n)]
ngrams = c.type.str.cat(others=shifted_cols, sep=" ")
ngrams.head()
```

0	i am 22 and
1	am 22 and i
2	22 and i have
3	and i have never
4	i have never had
	...
69933602	or webpage . hide
69933603	webpage . hide link
69933604	NaN
69933605	NaN
69933606	NaN

Name: type, Length: 69933607, dtype: object

The last three values in the Series are NaN because Pandas cannot concatenate three consecutive values to the types in these rows. NaN values can be replaced using the NaN replace (na_rep) argument. However, as NaNs interfere with counting, we will drop them using

```
ngrams = ngrams.dropna()
```

Next, to count all the four-gram types in the corpus, we will use value_counts().

```
ngram_counts = ngrams.value_counts()
ngram_counts.head()
```

type	
____	14026
. i do not	10683
? ? ? ?	9508
i do not know	5834
i do not think	5747

Name: count, dtype: int64

If we want to know the frequency of a specific *n*-gram, we can look it up in the ngram_counts Series using the dictionary lookup notation described earlier.

```
ngram_counts['on the other hand']
```

2724

Alternately, we can use the ngrams series and loc[] to locate *n*-grams that meet specific criteria. For example, one of the most frequent four-grams in this corpus is . *i do not* (beginning with a "."). We may wonder what typically comes

after this. To get a list of all four-grams that start with *i do not*, we use `loc []` with
`str.startswith()`.

```
idonot = ngrams.loc[ngrams.str.startswith("i do not")]
idonot.value_counts().head()
```

type

```
i do not know      5834
i do not think     5747
i do not want      2810
i do not have      2176
i do not see       1495
Name: count, dtype: int64
```

Earlier, we used `shift()` to examine the potential variable slot lexical bundle *on
the * hand*. We can use `str.contains()` and a regular expression for the same
purpose.

```
ngrams.loc[ngrams.str.contains('^on the .+ hand$')].\
value_counts()
```

type

```
on the other hand      2724
on the one hand        429
on the right hand      58
on the left hand       44
on the same hand       1
on the 2nd hand        1
on the first hand      1
on the invisible       1
   hand
on the wrong hand      1
on the engine hand     1
Name: count, dtype: int64
```

3.7.2 Context Windows

Many corpus-linguistic analyses require accounting for the immediate linguistic context around tokens of interest. However, up to this point, we have
dealt only superficially with context (for example, by finding and counting
the set of word types that occur immediately after personal pronouns). More
realistic use cases for dataframe corpora include analyzing words in context

or finding lists of collocates for one or more node words. In these cases (and others), it is necessary to adjust our unit of analysis from single word tokens to the linguistic environments around them – from tokens to context windows.

A context window is a small slice of a dataframe containing a predefined number of rows, usually *n* rows before and after a token of interest. There are several datatypes we might use to represent a context window in memory; each window could be a `list` or `Series` of row indices, or even `DataFrames` themselves. An excellent choice, however, is Python's `range`.

In Python, a `range` is a datatype like a `list` in that it contains multiple values, but it is more constrained in that it is defined by two values – one representing the lower bound of a sequence of integers, and the other representing the upper bound. Ranges are a useful datatype for representing context windows because context windows are always contiguous sequences of rows. Therefore, it is only necessary to store the lower and upper bounds of the window. Keeping a list of all the intermediary indices simply wastes memory. Ranges, irrespective of the size of the sequence of integers they cover, always take 48 bytes, but they can be indexed and sliced as if they contained the full set of integers. Additionally, ranges can be passed into the `loc[]` indexer without having to convert them to another datatype first. Consequently, ranges provide a fast, memory-efficient, and programmatically straightforward way to call up a context window on a corpus.

Ranges can be constructed as literals using the `range()` function.

```
range(10,15)
```

creates a `range` with a lower bound of 10 and an upper bound of 15. As with `lists`, ranges are zero-indexed. This means that the `range` just created includes the integers 10, 11, 12, 13, and 14, but not 15.

Therefore, if we want to create a context window around the row labeled 1000 with five rows before 1000 and five rows after 1000, we use

```
range(1000-5, 1+1000+5)
```

The extra 1 before the second argument is to offset Python's zero-based indexing. If we use a variable (`i`) instead of the number 1000, we use

```
range(i-5, 1+i+5)
```

Note that in cases where `i-5` is less than 0 or where `1+i+5` is greater than the number of rows in the `DataFrame`, some of the values in the range will not correspond to rows in the corpus. More on this in what follows.

If we have a `list` of indices we want to iterate over and create a context window for each, we can use a list comprehension.

```
indices=[10, 20, 30]
cws = [range(i-5, 1+i+5) for i in indices]
```

This is precisely the approach taken in the following code sample: first, we use the loc [] indexer to find all rows where the value in the lemma column is equal to *misinformation* and take the index of the resulting DataFrame. Then we use a list comprehension to create a range for each item in the index.

```
indices = c.loc[c.lemma.eq('misinformation')].index
cws = [range(index-5, 1+index+5) for index in indices]
```

We can test this by taking the first context window in cws and giving it to the loc [] indexer of our DataFrame.

```
c.loc[cws[0]]
```

	token	type	lemma	tag	pos	text	\
434236	is	is	be	VBZ	AUX	3243290	
434237	.	.	.	.	PUNCT	3243290	
434238	The	the	the	DT	DET	3243290	
434239	deluge	deluge	deluge	NN	NOUN	3243290	
434240	of	of	of	IN	ADP	3243290	
434241	misinformation	misinformation	misinformation	NN	NOUN	3243290	
434242	that	that	that	WDT	PRON	3243290	
434243	propagates	propagates	propagate	VBZ	VERB	3243290	
434244	that	that	that	IN	SCONJ	3243290	
434245	"	"	"	``	PUNCT	3243290	
434246	freelancing	freelancing	freelancing	NN	NOUN	3243290	

	register
434236	av
434237	av
434238	av
434239	av
434240	av
434241	av
434242	av
434243	av
434244	av
434245	av
434246	av

What we have produced is akin to a vertical Keyword in Context display for *misinformation*, but with additional information about each word.

Unfortunately, this approach still requires a bit of tuning. As noted earlier, this code will cause an error if index-5 is less than 0 or 1+index+5 is greater than the number of rows in the DataFrame. In these cases, Python looks for row labels that do not appear in the index and cannot find them (e.g., -1 or 100001 in a 100,000-token corpus). We can avoid this problem by slicing the `DataFrame` instead of passing the range directly into `loc[]`.

```
context_window = cws[0]
c.loc[context_window[0] : context_window[-1]]
```

Here, context_window[0] is the lower bound in the range; context_window[-1] is the upper bound. Including the : between them tells Python to slice the `DataFrame` instead of locating rows by their labels. This effectively avoids the problem.

More complex concordances can be created with a little more coding. We will also use context windows to create collocates lists. These procedures are discussed in Section 4.

3.8 Conclusion

In this section, we have discussed how to load, view, and export corpora stored in Pandas `DataFrames`; how to shift our unit of analysis from the token to the text or word type using `groupby()`; how to locate rows of interest based on one or more conditions; and how to focus our analysis on only those parts of the corpus that occur within a certain horizon around rows of interest using `loc[]`. These fundamental skills can be combined to complete a range of corpus linguistic tasks. In the next section, we will discuss how to use these skills to do common tasks such as construct concordances, analyze lexical bundles, and create lists of collocates.

4 Algorithms for Common Corpus Linguistic Tasks

4.1 A Brief Introduction to Algorithms

This section contains algorithms for five corpus linguistic procedures. These represent a small portion of the methods available to corpus linguists, but can be generalized to other tasks or extended to new procedures. For example, the lexical bundle algorithm (4.3) can be extended to a broad range of research questions regarding formulaic language. Thus, each algorithm is intended to focus on both a set of programming techniques and an area of CL analysis.

For this volume, I will adopt Hetland's definition of an algorithm as "a procedure, consisting of a finite set of steps (possibly including loops and conditionals) that solves a given problem in finite time" (Hetland, 2014, p. 10). In CL, the problems that algorithms solve involve reducing data in one form (the corpus) into another that captures something important about the sample (e.g., a concordance, a keyword list, a normalized frequency table). Therefore, it is helpful to think about (a) the state of the corpus before the first step of the algorithm – how the sample is structured and annotated, (b) what you intend the algorithm to produce (e.g., frequency counts, a list of collocates), and (c) the set of steps that will take the input in *a* and produce *b*.

Therefore, we will design algorithms in three broad stages:

1. specifying the desired output,
2. describing the form of the input, and
3. creating steps to produce the output given the input.

The last step can be further divided into

1. steps for inputting data,
2. steps for processing data, and
3. steps for producing output.

Each of these can also be broken down into more specific sets of steps. For example, the input step might be split into

1. import packages and functions,
2. load the corpus, and
3. assign initial values to variables.

When we have broken the problem down into instructions that a computer can follow, we have reached a desirable level of specificity. This might mean there is one line of code in the Python implementation for every line in the algorithm, but that is not always desirable. Rather, when you reach a level of specificity at which you know how to accomplish each step in code, your algorithm is specific enough.

Often, there are many ways to achieve the same outcome and picking the best algorithm is a matter of balancing memory use, speed, and time spent writing and debugging code. For functions you intend to reuse often, speed of execution might be your primary concern. For a function you intend to use one time, you may focus on saving time writing and debugging code at the cost of execution speed.

Specifying the Desired Output

Our first step in designing an effective algorithm is to specify the desired form of the output. Consider a collocates list. We would reasonably want to know the following information about each word that co-occurs with a node word:

1. raw frequency in the corpus,
2. frequency of co-occurrence with the node, and
3. a measure of strength of association between the two (e.g., Mutual Information, Z-score, logDice).

The output of this algorithm, therefore, might reasonably be a `DataFrame` where every row is one collocate, and each column is one piece of information about that collocate.

Specifying the form of the output of an algorithm requires choosing a unit of analysis (what the rows of a `DataFrame` are meant to represent). In the preceding collocates list example, the unit of analysis is the collocate *type*. In contrast, the unit of analysis for an algorithm meant to find the frequencies of a word in every text in the corpus might take the *text* as its unit of analysis (each row would correspond to one text in the corpus and each column to one type). The output of an algorithm meant to generate a concordance, on the other hand, would take the word *token* as its unit of analysis (each row would correspond to one occurrence of the word).

Specifying the Form of the Input

Given data of a certain form, an algorithm always produces the same result. However, given data of a different form (even slightly), the algorithm may break the execution of the program, or succeed, but produce a result that is different from that which was expected. Accordingly, every algorithm includes a set of assumptions about the state of the data that goes into the first step. These assumptions are sometimes referred to as the algorithm's *input conditions*. Assuming the input is always a dataframe with rows representing tokens, and columns for *token, type, text, lemma, tag, pos,* and *register* reduces the need to specify input conditions considerably, but there are still times when we will want to modify the dataframe in some way before the processing begins, for example, by removing function words before generating a collocates list, or adding a column for semantic tags prior to a keyword analysis.

Creating a Sequence of Steps to Process the Input and Produce the Output

The next step is to construct a sequence of operations that will complete the algorithm. As noted previously, there are often many ways to approach corpus-linguistic tasks, but it is generally a good idea to aim for clear, readable code where every step has a single, easily identifiable purpose. This not only helps with debugging, but also makes your code accessible to others who might need to check your work.

An Outline for the Rest of this Section

This section contains five additional sections – one each on algorithms for creating concordances, finding and analyzing lexical bundles, creating collocates lists, finding keywords, and performing key feature analysis. They were selected for inclusion here because they demonstrate important concepts in dataframe programming and, when examined in sequence, build on the previous algorithms. The linguistic and programming focuses for each algorithm appear in Table 4.

4.2 Creating a Concordance

The algorithm in this section finds all instances of one or more words or linguistic features and presents them with their immediate linguistic context (*L* preceding tokens and *R* following tokens) in a vertical format – one token in context per line. In other words, this algorithm produces a concordance. Concordances present instances of linguistic features vertically, centered on the linguistic feature of interest to facilitate comparison of context across repetitions. They are a core analytic tool for corpus linguists and thus, the first algorithm described here.

The output of the algorithm is a dataframe where each row represents one occurrence of the target word. The following algorithm produces a `DataFrame` where the first column has the lemma of the key word in the same row, and the remaining columns include the context to the left, the key word, and the context to the right.

The algorithm requires two types of input – the corpus to operate on (a `DataFrame` corpus with columns for, at least, `token` and `lemma`), and constants such as what to look for and the size of the left and right contexts. Since CORE is stored in the necessary format already, no additional processing is required to prepare it for the algorithm. The lemmas to search for are specified in a `list` of `strings`. The window size is specified in two integers – one for the size of the left context and one for the size of the right context.

Table 4 Linguistic and programming focuses for algorithms in Section 4.

Section	Algorithm	Linguistic focus	Programming focus
4.2	Concordances	Analyzing occurrences of words in linguistic context	Working with context windows, creating `DataFrames`
4.3	Lexical bundles	Analyzing formulaic language	Working with *n*-grams
4.4	Collocates	Analyzing lexical co-occurrence patterns	Vector-based mathematical operations
4.5	Keywords	Determining *aboutness* of a text or (sub)corpus	Grouping and applying functions
4.6	Key features	Text linguistic analysis of lexico-grammatical variation	Counting grammatical features, anonymous functions

In the input stage, the corpus is loaded into memory and the values of the constants are set. In the processing stage, all instances of the search terms are found, and context windows built around their indices. In the output stage, a new `DataFrame` in the form of the desired output is arranged and written to a .csv file. The steps of the algorithm are as follows:

Input

1. Import pandas.
2. Load the corpus.
3. Set search terms.
4. Set left and right context window sizes.

Processing

5. Filter the corpus.
6. Extract the indices of remaining rows.
7. Get context windows around each index.
8. Create a new `DataFrame` using the context windows.

Output

9. Rename columns to reflect distance from the key word.
10. Insert a lemma column at the start of the `DataFrame`.
11. Sort the `DataFrame` on the lemma column.
12. Export the `DataFrame` to an Excel spreadsheet.

And now in Python. We will search for instances of the semantically related words *fill*, *pour*, and *load*.

```python
# 1. Import pandas
import pandas as pd

# 2. Load the corpus
c = pd.read_pickle('CORE.pickle')

# 3. Create a list with our search terms
query = ['fill', 'pour', 'load']

# 4. Create two integer variables to represent left and
# right context window sizes
```

```
L = 3
R = 3

# 6. Extract the indices of those rows
indices = c.loc[c.lemma.isin(query)].index

# 7. Get context windows around each index
context_windows = [range(ind-L, 1+ind+R) for ind in indices]

# 8. Create a new DataFrame using a list of slices of the token
# column of the corpus
slices = [c.loc[cw[0]:cw[-1]].token.values
        for cw in context_windows]
df = pd.DataFrame(slices, index=indices)

# 9. Rename the columns to reflect distance from the key word
df.columns = range(-L, 1+R)

# 10. Insert a column at the start of the DataFrame with the
# lemma of the key word
df.insert(0, 'query', c.loc[indices].lemma.str.upper())

# 11. sort the DataFrame on the lemma column
df = df.sort_values(by='query')

# 12. export the DataFrame to an Excel spreadsheet
df.to_csv('concordance.csv', sep='\t')
```

Most of the preceding code is covered in the previous section, though it may be helpful to zoom in on steps 6–9 to look at how df, the dataframe with the concordance, is created. In steps 6 and 7, a list of context windows for the terms in query is generated according to the procedure in Section 3. Then, in step 8, a list of slices is extracted from c.token corresponding to the context windows. This is done with a list comprehension, which iterates over every context window in context_windows and extracts the content of the token column in that window as a Series.

It is necessary to extract just the values to avoid errors caused by mismatched indices. The index of the returned Series is identical to the index of the section of the DataFrame the Series was extracted from. Therefore, each element in the list comprehension has a different index because each context window looks upon a different section of the corpus. Differences in the indexes would cause problems if we tried to put all the `Series` together into a single dataframe, as Pandas will try to align the columns based on their indexes instead of their distance from the query term. It cannot do this, however, as none of the indices overlap. Consequently, every word in every slice would get its own column and `NaN` values would be filled into all the empty cells. We avoid this problem by dropping the indexes from the slices using the `values` property. As the name suggests, `values` returns an array of values without any meta-data – in this case, just the words in the `token` column without the index.

Also in step 8, `slices` is passed into `pd.DataFrame()` with the argument `index=indices`. This creates a new `DataFrame` where each column contains word tokens a certain distance from the query. The first column contains words that are L tokens to the left of the query. The second column contains items L-1 tokens to the left, and so on. To make this clear, we rename the columns in step 9.

In steps 10 and 11, we insert a column to record which lemma was in each context window and then sort the rows of the corpus based on that value. Finally in step 12, we write the concordance to a .csv file with tab characters delimiting columns.

To view the concordance, open the .csv file. If you would like to check that the algorithm produced the expected results, view the head of the output dataframe on the console.

```
df.head(3)
```

```
          query -3   -2     -1   0    1      2     3
7377      FILL  _    _      (    fill in     your  favorite
30225971  FILL  new  law    will fill in     the   "
30127595  FILL  you  think  to   fill it)leave them  a
```

The algorithm in this section demonstrates how to create a concordance. One benefit of the output being a dataframe is that it can be filtered, sorted, and otherwise manipulated using the methods described in Section 3. However, examining a concordance is often a step that comes after previous analyses that indicate which linguistic features to examine in the first place. In the next sections, therefore, we will explore algorithms that identify prominent lexical bundles and collocates for a target word. Both algorithms identify linguistic features that might be examined in more detail through a concordance.

Explore on your own!

1) Modify the algorithm to locate only rows where the next row has a noun POS tag (HINT: Modify step 6 to include multiple conditions in `loc[]`. `shift()` will also be helpful).

2) Next, modify the algorithm to locate only infinitives. Look for rows where the lemma of the preceding row is *to*.
3) Finally, add code to the algorithm to count the values at R1 for each of the lemmas using `groupby('query')` and `value_counts()`. Write the `Series` of frequency counts to a .csv file and look for patterns in the results.

4.3 Analyzing Lexical Bundles

Lexical bundles are frequently recurring n-grams that occur at a rate above a certain frequency threshold (e.g., 10 times per million words). Other structural and dispersion criteria have also been applied to the definition of lexical bundles. In their seminal study of university registers, for example, Biber, Conrad, and Cortes (2004) required bundles to occur at least 40 times per million words in at least five texts, and be sequences of four lexical items (thus, not including punctuation tokens).

Analysts are frequently interested in exploring the lexical bundles that characterize a register or other type of discourse. This often involves a two-step process of first finding and describing structural patterns in the most frequently recurring bundles and then investigating how those bundles function in discourse. The algorithm in this section demonstrates the first step in this process – creating a list of *n*-grams that conform to certain structural, frequency, and dispersion requirements. The algorithm demonstrates adding an *n*-gram column to the corpus and then producing a second `DataFrame` with frequency and range statistics for those *n*-grams that meet the requirements to be considered lexical bundles.

The input for the algorithm includes the corpus itself as a Pandas `DataFrame`, as well as the set of constants that will define our frequency and range cutoffs. We will follow Biber, Conrad, and Cortes (2004) in defining lexical bundles as sequences of four lexical tokens that occur at least 40 times per million words in at least 5 different texts. As we are defining lexical bundles as lexical four-grams (e.g., not including punctuation), we should also set a constant defining what we consider punctuation. Here, we will include only sentence punctuation (., ?, and !) and commas. As we are interested in functional interpretation, we will limit our analysis to a single register – interviews.

The output of the algorithm will be a `DataFrame` where each row represents one n-gram with columns for the normalized frequency (per million words) and text range of the n-gram in the corpus.

To start the algorithm, we import pandas, load the corpus, and set the values of the constants. The punctuation tokens will be held in a regular expression so that we can use `str.contains()` to filter out punctuation later. In the processing stage, we add an *n*-gram column to the corpus, filter on our three criteria, and then write the resulting `DataFrame` to a file and check the `head()`.

Input

1. Import pandas.
2. Load the corpus and create a subset of interviews.
3. Set constants.

Processing

4. Create an *n*-gram column and add it to the corpus.
5. Create a `DataFrame` of four-grams with columns for

   1. frequency, and
   2. text range.

6. Filter out *n*-grams that contain punctuation.
7. Filter out *n*-grams that do not occur at least 40 times per million words.
8. Filter out *n*-grams that do not occur in at least five texts.

Output

9. Sort the `DataFrame` on frequency and range.
10. Write to csv.
11. Check output with `head()`.

And now in Python. Note that the code comments are sparser than in the concordance algorithm.

```
# 1. import pandas
import pandas as pd

# 2. load corpus and extract interviews ('it')
c = pd.read_pickle('CORE.pickle')
c = c.loc[c.register.eq('it')]

# 3. set constants
min_freq = 40
min_range = 5
punct = r'[.,?!]'
```

```
# 4. add four_gram column to corpus
shifted_cols = [c.type.shift(-i) for i in range(1, 4)]
c['four_gram'] = c.type.str.cat(
        others=shifted_cols, sep=' ')


# 5. create DataFrame with frequency and range information
df = pd.DataFrame({
    'freq': c.four_gram.value_counts() / (c.shape[0]-3),
    'range': c.groupby('four_gram').text.nunique()})
df.freq = df.freq * 1000000


# 6. filter ngrams that cross punc boundaries
df = df.loc[~(df.index.str.contains(punct))]


# 7. filter ngrams that occur fewer than 40 times per million
# words
df = df.loc[df.freq.ge(min_freq)]


# 8. filter ngrams that occur in fewer than 5 texts
df = df.loc[df.range.ge(min_range)]


# Output
# 9. sort df on freq, range
df = df.sort_values(by=['freq', 'range'],
ascending=False)


# 10. write to .csv
df.to_csv('lexical_bundles.csv', sep='\t')


# 11. check output
df.head()
```

	freq	range
four_gram		
i do not know	264.169188	86
i do not think	196.050089	79
do not want to	181.097116	62
i think it 's	142.883963	64
to be able to	116.300900	48

In the preceding algorithm, the `four_gram` column is created using `str.cat()` and `shift()`. Then a four-gram frequency dataframe is created in step 5. Frequency counts are normalized by dividing the raw frequencies of the four-grams by the number of four-grams in the corpus (equal to the number of tokens in the corpus – 3) and then multiplied by one million. The `df` is then filtered using the `loc[]` indexer, `contains()`, and `ge()`. The first two are described in Section 3, but `ge()` is new. The `ge()` function works exactly as `eq()`, but returns `True` for values that are greater than or equal to its argument.

The algorithm in this section demonstrates how to identify lexical bundles for a corpus, but the core of the procedure can be applied to a range of concepts where the unit of analysis is fundamentally a sequence of tokens. Indeed, *n*-grams provide a convenient starting point for phraseological analyses of multitoken units such as compounds and phrasal verbs, formulaic language, and verb-argument constructions.

Explore on your own!

1) *i do not know* is the most frequent lexical bundle in interviews. Create a concordance for the bundle, write it to a .csv file, and examine the results. What discourse functions are accomplished with it?
2) Choose another register in CORE and compare/contrast the functions of *i do not know* in that register and interviews. Consider advice (av) or opinion blogs (ob) for the comparison register.
3) Choose one or more lexical bundle from your list. Investigate the possibility of it having variable slots. Use the techniques in Section 3.7.1.

4.4 Finding Collocates

Linguists are often interested in generating a list of collocates for a node word – those words which co-occur with the node more often than might be expected. A range of measures of the collocation strength between the node and words that co-occur with it have been proposed (see, e.g., Brezina, 2018 for a comparison of 14 measures). Most measures of collocation strength, however, cannot be compared across corpora. LogDice (Rychlý, 2008), however, does permit comparisons across corpora. In this algorithm, we find logDice values for collocates of *misinformation* in CORE's news register. We then compare the values of some of the top collocates to see if the collocation strength differs in news compared to the opinion blogs register.

Calculating logDice involves three steps:

1. counting the word types in the corpus to establish base frequencies,
2. finding how often each word occurs in a window around instances of the node (its observed frequency of collocation), and
3. using those frequencies to calculate Log Dice with Eq. (1)

$$LogDice = 14 + \log_2 \frac{2 \times f_{xy}}{f_x + f_y} \tag{1}$$

where f_{xy} is the observed frequency of co-occurrence, f_x is the frequency of the node word, and f_y is the frequency of the potential collocate.

The output of the algorithm is a `DataFrame` with each row representing one word type in the corpus. We include columns for the raw frequency of the word in the corpus (`Y`), the observed frequency of collocation (`O`), and the Log Dice score (`LD`).

The input for the algorithm includes

1. the corpus – a Pandas `DataFrame` with (at least) a column for `type`,
2. the identity of the node word (a string). Here, we will find collocates for *misinformation* in the news register,
3. the size of the window around the node to examine (two `integers`), and
4. the minimum corpus frequency and frequency of co-occurrences for words to be considered potential collocates (two `integers`).

To start the algorithm, we will load the corpus and set the values of all constants (e.g., the window size and frequency cutoffs). In the processing stage, we will calculate the observed frequencies of co-occurrence, and calculate logDice values. Finally, in the output stage, we will apply frequency cutoffs, and export the resulting `DataFrame` to a .csv file.

Input

1. Import Pandas and the `log2` function from NumPy.
2. Load the corpus and select only news texts.
3. Create string to represent the node.
4. Create integer variables to represent

   1. left and right context window sizes, and
   2. the base frequency cut-off and observed collocation frequency cutoff.

Processing

5. Get frequency counts for all word types in the corpus.

6. Get the indices of all instances of the node in the corpus using `loc`.
7. Create context windows from the indices.
8. Create a flat list of indices in all context windows (with duplicates).
9. Create a `Series` with the frequencies of all word types that occur in the context windows.
10. Calculate logDice.

Output

11. Create a `DataFrame` with columns for base frequency, observed frequency of collocation, and logDice score.
12. Filter out rows with frequency values below the cut-offs as well as the node (so it is not considered a collocate of itself).
13. Sort the `DataFrame` by logDice scores in descending order.
14. Export the `DataFrame` to a .csv file.
15. Check the output with `head()`.

And now the algorithm implemented in Python:

```
## INPUT
# 1. import pandas and the log2 function from numpy
import pandas as pd
from numpy import log2

# 2. load the corpus and select the tokens from texts of the
# news (ne) register
c = pd.read_pickle('CORE.pickle')
c = c.loc[c.register.eq('ne')]

# 3. create string to represent the node (node)
node = 'misinformation'

# 4. create integer variables to represent the context window
# and freq cut-offs
L = 5
R = 5
freq_cut = 5
coll_cut = 5

## PROCESSING
# Get Observed Frequencies
# 5. get frequencies of all word types
Y = c.type.value_counts()
```

```
# 6. get indices of node in the corpus
indices = c.loc[c.lemma.eq(node)].index

# 7. create context windows from the indices
cws = [range(ind-L, 1+ind+R) for ind in indices]

# 8. create a flat list of indices in all context windows (with
# duplicates)
cw_indices = [ind for cw in cws for ind in cw]

# 9. create a Series with the frequencies of all word types
# that occur in the context windows
O = c.loc[cw_indices].type.\
cat.remove_unused_categories().value_counts()

# 10. get log Dice
LD = 14 + log2((2*O) / (Y+Y.loc[node]))


## OUTPUT
# 11. create an Output DataFrame
df = pd.DataFrame({'Y': Y,
                   'O': O,
                   'logDice': LD})

# 12. filter out rows: the node and words with frequency values
# below the cut-off
df = df.drop(node)
df = df.loc[df.Y.ge(freq_cut) & df.O.ge(coll_cut)]

# 13. sort the DataFrame by Log Dice score in descending order
df = df.sort_values(by='logDice', ascending=False)

# 14. export the DataFrame to an Excel file
df.to_csv('collocates of misinformation in news.csv',
        sep='\t')

# 15. check output
df.head(3)
```

	Y	O	logDice
type			
lies	587	10.0	8.977632
about	26698	10.0	3.614084
so	23950	5.0	2.770400

The statement importing log2() from NumPy in step 1 begins with the from keyword. This allows us to import only a single function (or a small set of functions) instead of the entire library. The log2() function calculates base 2 logarithms and is used in step 10 to calculate logDice.

In step 5, a Series with frequency counts for every word type in the corpus is created. These are the Y values in the preceding formula. In steps 6–8, the indices of the node are extracted and used to generate context windows. A list comprehension is used in step 7 to flatten the list of indices in the context windows produced in step 6 – transforming it from a 2-dimensional list of lists of indices to a one-dimensional list of indices. The flattened list is then passed into loc[] in step 8, which returns a DataFrame with those rows that are in one or more context windows. Words that occur in multiple context windows are included multiple times. Then, value_counts() is used in step 9 to count all the values in the type column of the context windows around the node. This produces observed frequencies of co-occurrence for all types in all context windows and stores them in a Series called O. The cat. remove_unused_categories() in step 9 is necessary to remove word types from the index of the Series for those words that occur in the corpus, but not in a context window around an instance of the node. If we do not remove these, their observed frequencies of 0 will cause an error when Log Dice is calculated in step 10.

Log Dice is calculated using vector-based math operations according to the preceding formula. The entire Series O is multiplied by the scalar 2. The result is divided by the sum of the Series Y (corpus frequencies of all words) and the corpus frequency of the node (retrieved from the Series Y using Y.loc[node]). Finally, the result is logged using the log2() function imported in step 1. In step 10, 14 is added to the result of log2(). There is no need to add, multiply, divide, or log individual values. The operations +, *, \ and log2() all work on the entire Series at once.

Finally, in steps 11, 12, and 13, a DataFrame with frequencies, frequencies of co-occurrence, and logDice scores is created and filtered according to the frequency and co-occurrence cutoffs set in step 4.

The results indicate that the top collocate of *misinformation* in news is *lies* with a logDice score of 8.978. One might wonder if this is true in other registers. By changing 'ne' to 'ob' in step 2 (one might also want to change the name of the output file), we can find collocates of *misinformation* in opinion blogs. Results indicate that *lies* is also a collocate of *misinformation* in that register (logDice = 7.69), but the strength of association is not as great. The difference indicates that *lies* co-occurs with *misinformation* more than twice as often in news than in opinion blogs. On the other hand, the top collocate in opinion blogs is *spread* (logDice = 8.18), which has a logDice value of 7.2 in news. These differences may (or may not) point to differences in the discourse around misinformation in the two registers.

The algorithm demonstrated here is flexible enough to be extended to any corpus-linguistic analysis that relies on measuring association between linguistic items. Modifying one or more of steps 3 through 10 allows analysts to apply a different established measure of strength of association (e.g., Cohen's *d*; z-scores), or test a new one. Alternately, strength of association can be calculated between different types of linguistic items (e.g., word type and part of speech tag; variable slot lexical bundle and slot fillers). Further, the output can be used to identify peculiar combinations of word types that may be investigated with close analysis of a concordance.

Explore on your own!

1) Some strength of association measures require the analyst to calculate a word type's expected frequency (e.g., Mutual Information; z-score). This can be done by multiplying the frequency of the node by the frequency of the collocate and dividing the result by the number of words in the corpus. Modify the algorithm to use z-scores instead of logDice by subtracting expected values from Y and dividing the result by the square root of the expected values (import the sqrt() function from numpy).

2) Compare the lists created using the two measures of strength of association. Does one appear intuitively superior to the other?

3) Choose a collocate of *misinformation* from one of the two lists. Modify the concordance algorithm to produce a concordance for co-occurrences of the node and collocate. Use the node as your query. After the slices are extracted, but before the dataframe is created, add

a line of code to filter out slices that do not include the collocate. Drop the `index=indices` parameter from the `DataFrame()` function in the next line to prevent an error.

4.5 Keyword Analysis Using Text-Dispersion Keyness

Keywords are often identified by comparing their prominence in one corpus to their prominence in a second, usually larger corpus (these corpora are referred to in what follows as the *focal* and *reference* corpora respectively). Though many metrics for measuring this prominence (or *keyness*) of key-words have been proposed (see e.g., Gabrielatos, 2018), recent research suggests that comparing word types' dispersion across texts in focal and reference corpora produces readily interpretable keyword lists (Egbert & Biber, 2019). This measure of keyness has been called *text-dispersion key-ness* (hereafter, TDK).

TDK is calculating in three steps. First, a list of all word types in the focal corpus is generated and the range of each type is found (the number of texts in the corpus in which the type appears). Then, the number of texts in the reference corpus that contain each type is found. These numbers, along with the total number of texts in each corpus is used to calculate G^2, a log-likelihood ratio (LLR). Keywords can then be ranked according to their LLR value. Alternatively, LLRs may be compared to a critical value where LLRs greater than certain thresholds indicate statistically significant differences in strength of association at various p-values. Table 5 is reproduced from Paul Rayson's online log-likelihood calculator[1] (Rayson, n.d.).

Formulae for computing LLRs appear in several sources, but the seminal text is Dunning (1993). Equation (2) is presented in Egbert and Biber (2019, p. 84).

$$G^2 = 2 \sum_i O_i ln\left(\frac{O_i}{E_i}\right) \qquad (2)$$

The values of i represent the focal and reference corpora. O_i is the range of the word in the corpus and E_i is the expected range, which can be calculated according to Eq.(3):

$$E_i = \frac{N_i \sum_i O_i}{\sum_i N_i} \qquad (3)$$

where N_i is the number of texts in either corpus.

[1] *Log-likelihood and effect size calculator.* http://ucrel.lancs.ac.uk/llwizard.html

Table 5 LLR critical values

LLR Critical Value	*p*-Value
3.84	$p < 0.05$
6.63	$p < 0.01$
10.83	$p < 0.001$
15.13	$p < 0.0001$

An algorithm for finding LLRs thus requires the range of the target word in the focal corpus (O_{foc}) the range of the word in the reference corpus (O_{ref}), the number of texts in the focal corpus (N_{foc}), and the number of texts in the reference corpus (N_{ref}). In the processing stage, the algorithm calculates expected values for both corpora and then uses the observed and expected values to calculate the LLR, which is printed in the output stage.

Input

1. Import log from math
2. Set value for O_foc, O_ref, N_foc, and N_ref

Processing

3. Get expected values
4. Calculate LLRs

Output

5. Print LLR to console

And now in Python. The code sample calculates the LLR for the word *misinformation* in news compared to a reference corpus consisting of the other CORE registers. The values of O_foc (observed range in news), O_ref (observed range in other registers), N_foc (number of texts in news), N_ref (number of texts in other registers) are set as constants here, but obtained programmatically in the next algorithm.

```
## Input
from math import log

# set observed values
O_foc = 63
O_ref = 199
N_foc = 10069877
```

```
N_ref = 51168525


## Processing
# get expected values
E_foc = N_foc * (O_foc + O_ref) / (N_foc + N_ref)
E_ref = N_ref * (O_foc + O_ref) / (N_foc + N_ref)


# get llr
llr = 2 * ((O_foc * log(O_foc / E_foc)) +
           (O_ref * log(O_ref / E_ref)))


## Output
print(llr)
```

9.916901839587666

The LLR for *misinformation* is about 9.9, indicating that it is the keyword for news. To get a sense of the topics in the news subcorpus, however, we will need a much more extensive list of keywords. We can obtain this by applying the LLR algorithm to every type in the corpus and then filtering out those types with LLR values below a critical value of 3.84 or higher depending on the desired *p*-value.

We can accomplish this by creating a dataframe where the unit of analysis is the type (i.e., each row represents one word type) with columns for range in the focal corpus and range in the reference corpus. Then, we may convert the LLR algorithm into a function and `apply()` it to each row in the new `DataFrame`. The `apply()` function is a useful one that allows a coder to apply a function to each column or row in a `DataFrame`. It is discussed in more detail in the following discussion.

We now have (nearly) all the tools necessary to complete the full algorithm.

Input

1. Load libraries.
2. Load corpus.
3. Filter out punctuation.
4. Define log-likelihood function.

Processing

5. Create subcorpora.
6. Create a `DataFrame` with ranges for every word in the corpora.
7. Replace ranges of 0 with ranges of 0.5.
8. Apply the log-likelihood function to each row.

9. Filter out rows with LLR < 3.84 and sort the `DataFrame`.
10. Write the `DataFrame` to a .csv file.
11. Check output using `head()`.

Step 7 is necessary; if the observed range of a word in the reference corpus is 0, the LLR function will fail because the natural logarithm of 0 is negative infinity. To avoid this, we might filter out words that do not occur in one of the two subcorpora, but this will cause us to miss words that occur frequently in the focal corpus but not at all in the reference. The solution here, changing values of 0 to 0.5, is taken from Rayson (n.d.), but other solutions are possible.

```
# 1. import libraries
import pandas as pd
from math import log

# 2. read corpus
c = pd.read_pickle('CORE.pickle')

# 3. filter out punctuation
c = c.loc[~c.pos.eq('PUNCT')]

# 4. define Log Likelihood Function
def LLR(row, a, b):
        # set observed values
        O_foc = row.foc
        O_ref = row.ref
        N_foc = a
        N_ref = b

        # get expected values
        E_foc = N_foc * (O_foc + O_ref) / (N_foc + N_ref)
        E_ref = N_ref * (O_foc + O_ref) / (N_foc + N_ref)

        # get llr
        llr = 2 * ((O_foc * log(O_foc / E_foc)) +
                   (O_ref * log(O_ref / E_ref)))
```

```
            # return LLR
            return llr


# 5. create subcorpora


# create focal corpus by selecting news texts
# and get the number of texts in the subcorpus
foc = c.loc[c.register.eq('ne')]
N_foc = foc.text.nunique()


# create reference corpus by selecting non-news texts
# and get the number of texts
ref = c.loc[~c.register.eq('ne')]
N_ref = ref.text.nunique()


# 6. create output dataframe with foc and ref ranges
foc_counts = foc.value_counts(['type','text']).\
        groupby(level='type').count()
ref_counts = ref.value_counts(['type','text']).\
        groupby(level='type').count()
df = pd.DataFrame({'foc': foc_counts, 'ref': ref_counts})


# 7. replace range counts of 0 with 0.5s to avoid log(0)
# errors in the LLR function
df.foc = df.foc.mask(df.foc.eq(0), 0.5)
df.ref = df.ref.mask(df.ref.eq(0), 0.5)


# 8. create log likelihood ratio column with apply()
df['llr'] = df.apply(LLR, args=[N_foc, N_ref], axis=1)


# 9. filter out values and sort
df = df.loc[df.llr > 3.84]
df.sort_values('llr', ascending=False, inplace=True)


# 10. output
df.to_csv('tdk ne keywords.csv', sep='\t')


# 11. check head
df.head()
```

	foc	ref	llr
type			
said	6701.0	12248.0	1935.629401
mr	1392.0	1474.0	1029.995499
president	1953.0	2777.0	944.980129
your	3592.0	21819.0	881.697414
government	2881.0	5198.0	859.024513

These first five keywords point to the discourse of news and its characteristic functions and topics (e.g., reporting speech, government).

There are three new elements in the preceding algorithm: using the `def` keyword to define the LLR function, using `value_counts()` and `groupby()` to get text ranges for each type in the corpora, and using `apply()` to apply the LLR function to each row in the corpus. Each deserves additional explanation.

At the top of the code, after the import statements, the function `LLR()` is defined using the `def` keyword. The next eight lines (not including comments) are indented. This indicates that these lines will be executed when `LLR()` is called. The content of this function is identical to the content of the algorithm for finding LLR. However, note that this function takes three arguments (`row`, `a`, and `b`) and these are used to set the observed values that were constants in the original algorithm (more on these arguments in a moment).

In step 6, a `DataFrame` is created with two columns: one each for the ranges of each word type in the focal and reference corpora. The ranges for the focal corpus are calculated with `foc.value_counts(['type', 'text'])`. `groupby(level='type').count()`. Three methods are chained here. First, frequencies for each type in each text are calculated with `value_counts(['type', 'text'])`. Note that the use of `value_counts()` differs slightly here compared to its use in previous algorithms. It is invoked on the `DataFrame` instead of a column, and a list of column names is passed into the method. Passing a list of column names to `value_counts()` produces a hierarchical list of counts.

```
foc.value_counts(['type', 'text'])
```

type	text	
the	0737349	5679
	0163670	3169
of	0737349	2730
to	0737349	2530
the	1718796	2406

```
                          . . .
matter        3226900     1
              3287602     1
              3377852     1
              0044209     1
percentage    0069238     1
Name: count, Length: 3801200, dtype: int64
```

The datatype of the result is a Series, not a DataFrame, but note that the index of the Series has two levels; one for type and one for text. The output thus indicates that *the* occurs 5,679 times in text 0737349 and 3,169 in text 0163670 (note that the Series is sorted in descending order). groupby(level='type') then organizes the rows of the Series into groups (one for each word type). count() after groupby() returns the number of values within each group (here, there is one value for each text in each group), so grouping by type and counting the resulting values per group produces the range of each word type.

In step 8, the LLR() function defined at the start of the algorithm is applied to each row of df using df.apply(LLR, args=[N_foc, N_ref], axis=1). Since df is indexed by word type, LLRs are found for each word type. The first argument passed to apply() is the name of a function with no trailing parentheses (in this case, LLR). The second argument (args=[N_foc, N_ref]) is a list of any variables to pass into the function as arguments in addition to the rows of the dataframe (in this case, the number of tokens in the foc and ref dataframes). The last argument for apply(), axis=1 indicates that the function should be applied to the rows of the dataframe instead of columns. apply() can apply a function to the columns of a DataFrame by omitting the axis=1 argument.

Careful readers may notice that the line def LLR(row, a, b): in step 4 suggests that the LLR function takes three arguments, but the list in args= [N_foc, N_ref] in step 9 includes only two values. This is because the first argument in the function is always the rows of the DataFrame. So, df.apply (LLR, args=[N_foc, N_ref], axis=1) has the following effect. First, it iterates over the rows in df. For each row, it calls the LLR() function and passes three arguments: the current row (as a Series), the number of texts in the focal corpus (N_foc), and the number of texts in the reference corpus (N_ref). For each row, LLR() returns a value, which apply() concatenates into a Series. This series is added to df with the column name *llr* with the assignment operator =.

In the final two steps, the data are filtered, sorted, and written to a file, and the head is displayed to the console.

The algorithm in this section demonstrates keyword analysis but is more generally designed to demonstrate grouping and hierarchical counting, as well as row-wise application of functions. These techniques are widely useful for a range of corpus linguistic tasks that require the analyst to transform a `DataFrame` so that the rows represent something other than tokens. In the final algorithm of this section, the unit of analysis is shifted fully to the text to facilitate analysis of grammatical structures in the sports reports subcorpus.

Explore on your own!

1) Modify the algorithm so that LLRs are calculated using corpus frequency instead of text range. Refer to the collocation algorithm for methods for getting corpus frequencies. Compare the keyword lists. In your opinion, does one list characterize the discourse of news better than the other?
2) Transform your keyword, collocation, and concordance algorithms into functions using `def`. Pay attention to the arguments that must be passed in and the return values of the functions.
3) Choose another register (e.g., sports reports – "sr") and generate a list of keywords for that register. Then, choose a set of words that are key in both registers and investigate their collocates. How do the collocations differ across registers?

4.6 Key Feature Analysis

The previous algorithms have focused on lexical items. However, many CL procedures focus on (lexico-)grammar. Key Feature Analysis (KF Analysis), for example (see e.g., Egbert & Biber, 2023), involves comparing the frequency of grammatical features across texts in two corpora to identify features that are relatively common in each (the key features). After identification, functional interpretations of the key features are made using close analysis of texts or concordance lines.

In this section, we replicate part of Egbert and Biber (2023)'s first case study – analyzing functional lexico-grammatical features in the register of sports reports by comparing normalized frequencies in that register to those of all other registers in CORE. In the case study, the authors selected 15 functional lexical and lexico-grammatical features for analysis:

- Second-person pronouns
- Third-person pronouns
- Activity verbs

- Adjectives
- Adverbs of place
- Common nouns
- Contractions
- Human nouns
- Nominalizations
- Past tense
- Perfect aspect
- Passive voice
- Premodifying nouns
- Proper nouns
- Word length

For our replication, we will drop the three semantic categories (activity verbs, adverbs of place, and human nouns) as well as word length, as the focus of this section is grammar.

Egbert and Biber propose Cohen's d as a measure of keyness for features due to the ease of calculation and interpretability. In KF Analysis, Cohen's d is the standardized mean difference in frequency of lexico-grammatical structures in two corpora. A feature with a d value of 1 occurs 1 standard deviation more often in the first corpus than the second. It may be calculated using Eq. (4).

$$d = \frac{M_1 - M_2}{SD_{pooled}} \qquad (4)$$

where M_1 and M_2 are the mean rates of occurrence of a linguistic feature in two corpora and SD_{pooled} (see Eq. (5)) is an estimate of the combined variance of the two sets of observations.

$$SD_{pooled} = \sqrt{\frac{SD_1^2 + SD_2^2}{2}} \qquad (5)$$

In (5), SD_1 and SD_2 are the standard deviations of the rates of occurrence for the feature in the two corpora. As we did for LLRs in the keyword analysis algorithm, we can write a function for Cohen's d and apply() it to a DataFrame. As Cohen's d is calculated with mean frequencies, however, it is necessary to calculate normalized frequencies on a per-text basis. This shifts the unit of analysis from the token (as in the concordance algorithm) or the type (as in the n-grams, collocation, and keywords algorithms) to the text. Thus, to perform KF Analysis, we will need to create a DataFrame for each corpus (one for sports reports and one for other registers) where rows correspond to texts and the columns correspond to the lexico-grammatical features that are central to the analysis. The cells in these dataframes should contain normalized frequency counts for each feature in each text. The output should be a `Series` of features with *d* values.

A basic algorithm for KF Analysis thus follows these steps.

Input

1. Import libraries and functions.
2. Define Cohen's *d* function.
3. Load corpus and filter out punctuation.

Processing

4. Create "counts" `DataFrame` with per-text frequencies of lexico-grammatical structures.
5. Normalize frequencies in counts.
6. Split the `DataFrame` into counts for sports reports and counts for other texts.
7. Apply Cohen's *d* function to the columns of the two counts dataframes.
8. Filter out low-magnitude values.

Output

9. Write results to file and check results on the console.

As always, we have already discussed most of the tools and procedures necessary to complete this algorithm. However, it is worth noting that counting grammatical features is not as simple as counting word types. Locating grammatical features involves the use of the `tag` and `pos` columns, often in conjunction with `lemma` and `type`. It is often not sufficient to rely on only one type of information. Locating third-person pronouns, for example, requires locating values of PRON or PRP in the pos or tag column, but then filtering out first- and second-person pronouns using information in the `lemma` column.

```
prp_3rd = c.loc[c.pos.eq('PRON') & c.lemma.isin([
  'they', 'she', 'he', 'it', 'one', 'these', 'those',
  'that', 'themselves', 'herself', 'himself', 'itself',
  'oneself'])]
prp_3rd.head(3)
```

	token	type	lemma	tag	pos	text	register
135	they	they	they	PRP	PRON	1465224	av
327	it	it	it	PRP	PRON	1465224	av
337	it	it	it	PRP	PRON	1465224	av

How you set the conditions in `loc[]` will reflect how you have operationalized the grammatical structures of interest (reference grammars may be of use
in operationalizing many structures). Many grammatical features can be
located using some combination of coarse-grained part-of-speech tags
(`pos`), fine-grained part-of-speech tags (`tag`), lemmas, and word
`types`. Additionally, properties of the tokens immediately before or after
a token of interest can be accessed through `shift()`. Pandas `str.`
`startswith()`, `str.endswith()`, and `str.contains()` methods
can be used to locate any of a set of tokens, types, or part-of-speech tags that
follows a prespecified pattern. Token and POS-tag *n*-grams can also be used
to find multiword grammatical structures. Context windows can be used to
count grammatical structures when some level of additional parsing is necessary, but doing so is outside the scope of the current volume.

Once located with `loc[]`, per-text frequency counts for grammatical
structures can be found by counting the values in the `text` column. Note
that `text.value_counts()` produces a `DataFrame` where rows correspond to texts. Consequently, the resulting dataframe can be used for this
analysis and others where the unit of analysis is the text.

```
counts = prp_3rd.text.value_counts().\
    sort_index(ascending=False).head(3)
```

```
text
3798147 10
3751580 25
3379896 29
Name: count, dtype: int64
```

The results indicate that text 3798147 has 10 third-person pronouns while text
3751580 has 25. We must divide these counts by the number of tokens in the text
to normalize them.

```
tokens_per_text = c.text.value_counts()
counts = counts / tokens_per_text * 1000
counts.sort_index(ascending=False).head(3)
```

```
text
3798147  13.315579
```

```
3751580   22.583559
3379896   23.673469
Name: count, dtype: float64
```

Third-person pronouns occur at a rate of about 13 per thousand words in text 3798147. Pandas automatically aligned the indices of the two `Series` so that counts for each text are divided by the number of words for the same text. This works when dividing one `Series` by another `Series` with identical indices. We now have a column with normalized frequency counts for one of the 11 features we wish to include in our KF analysis. Counting the other 10 features is just like counting this one, but with different conditions in `loc[]`. We are now ready to examine the full algorithm in Python.

```
# 1. import pandas and numpy
import pandas as pd
import numpy as np


# 2. def Cohen's d function
def cohen(x, y):

    # get estimate of pooled variance
    pooled = np.sqrt((x.std()**2 + y.std()**2)/2)

    # get standardized mean difference d
    d = (x.mean() - y.mean()) / pooled

    # return d
    return d


# 3. load corpus and remove punctuation
c = pd.read_pickle('CORE.pickle')
c = c.loc[~c.pos.eq('PUNCT')]


# 4. Create counts dataframe

# 4.1 set list of 3rd person pronouns
prp_3rd = ['they', 'she', 'he', 'it', 'one', 'these',
    'those', 'that', 'themselves', 'herself', 'himself',
    'itself', 'oneself']


# 4.2 set regular expression pattern for locating words with
# common nominalization endings
nom_pat = (r'.+ment$|.+ation$|.+ist$|.+ee$|.+ery$|'+
```

```
        r'.+age$|.+ness$|.+ity$|.+dom$|.+ship$|.+hood$|'+
        r'.+ite$|.+ish$|.+ism')


# 4.3 create df 'counts' with raw frequency of
# lexicogrammatical features
prop = c.loc[c.pos.eq('PROPN')].text.value_counts()
th_pp = c.loc[c.pos.eq('PRON') &
        c.lemma.isin(prp_3rd)].text.value_counts()
se_pp = c.loc[c.lemma.eq('you')].text.value_counts()
past = c.loc[c.tag.eq('VBD')].text.value_counts()
perf = c.loc[c.tag.eq('VBN') &
        c.lemma.shift(1).eq('have') &
        c.pos.shift(1).eq('AUX')].text.value_counts()
cont = c.loc[c.type.str.contains("'.{1,2}$")].\
        text.value_counts()
passive = c.loc[c.tag.eq('VBN') &
        c.lemma.shift(1).eq('be') &
        c.pos.shift(1).eq('AUX')].text.value_counts()
premod = c.loc[c.tag.str.startswith('N') &
        c.tag.shift(-1).str.startswith('N')].\
        text.value_counts()
adj = c.loc[c.tag.str.startswith('J')].\
        text.value_counts()
common = c.loc[c.tag.str.startswith('N') &
        ~c.tag.isin(['NNP', 'NNPS'])].\
        text.value_counts()
nom = c.loc[c.type.str.contains(nom_pat) &
        c.tag.str.startswith('N')].text.value_counts()


counts = pd.DataFrame({
        'Proper Nouns': prop,
        '3rd Person Pronouns': th_pp,
        '2nd Person Pronouns': se_pp,
        'Past Tense': past,
        'Perfect Aspect': perf,
        'Contractions': cont,
        'Passive Voice': passive,
        'Premodifying Nouns': premod,
        'Adjectives': adj,
        'Common Nouns': common,
        'Nominalizations': nom})
```

```
# 5. normalize counts to per 1000 words
text_lengths = c.text.value_counts()
counts = counts.apply(lambda col: col / text_lengths * 1000)

# 6. create subcorpora for comparison
sr_texts = c.loc[c.register.eq('sr')].text.unique()
sports = counts.loc[sr_texts]

ot_texts = c.loc[~c.register.eq('sr')].text.unique()
others = counts.loc[ot_texts]

# 7. calculate cohen's d
result = sports.apply(lambda col:
        cohen(col, others[col.name]))

# 8. filter out low magnitude values
cutoff = .2
result = result.loc[result.abs() > cutoff]
result = result.sort_values()

# 9. write results to csv
result.to_csv('key features of sports reports.csv')
print(result)
```

```
Common Nouns             -0.838475
Nominalizations          -0.778753
2nd Person Pronouns      -0.551680
Adjectives               -0.421875
Passive Voice            -0.334396
Premodifying Nouns        0.215672
3rd Person Pronouns       0.272039
Perfect Aspect            0.317762
Contractions              0.437526
Past Tense                0.515931
Proper Nouns              0.657777
```

dtype: float64

In steps 1 and 2, packages are imported and a function for computing Cohen's *d* is defined (cohen()). The function takes two arguments, x and y. These should be Pandas Series. The cohen() function calculates and returns the standardized mean difference for two Series according to the preceding formulae. In step 3, the corpus is loaded, and punctuation is dropped by selecting only rows where `pos` does not equal `PUNCT` (punctuation). In step 4, the `counts` dataframe is created with frequency counts for the 11 features of interest. Steps 4.1 and 4.2 set values to help with counting third-person pronouns and nominalizations. In 4.1, a list of third-person pronouns is created, and in step 4.2 a string is created with a regular expression pattern to find word types with common nominalization endings. As described earlier, regular expressions provide a system for matching strings based on patterns instead of matching literal characters. The pattern `.+ment$`, for example, matches all strings that end in *-ment*. The `|` is equivalent to "or", so `.+ment$|.+ation$|.+ist$` matches values that end in *-ment, -ation,* or *-ist*. The full pattern contains 14 nominalization endings, but will produce results with some error. For example, *nation* will be matched, as will *gist*, though neither of these is a nominalization. Nominalizations with endings not in the list (e.g., *-al*) will be passed over; the program will not catch *refusal*. In step 4.3, the counts `DataFrame` is created with columns for each of the 11 features included in our KF analysis.

A variable is created for each feature with a statement in the form of `c.loc[...].text.value_counts()` with a unique set of conditions in the `loc[]` indexer. For finding proper nouns, the sole condition is `c.pos.eq('PROPN')`. In contrast, three conditions are included for finding passive voice verbs: the `tag` must contain a past participle verb tag (`c.tag.eq('VBN')`), the `lemma` column in the preceding row must be a *be* verb (`c.lemma.shift(1).eq('be')`), and the `pos` column of the preceding row must be an auxiliary verb tag (`c.pos.shift(1).eq('AUX')`). A `DataFrame` is then created with columns for each feature.

In step 5, the frequencies in `counts` are normalized to a rate of 1,000 words. In previous examples, `Series` of frequency counts were divided by the number of words in each text. One might assume that this procedure will work with a `DataFrame` as well, but it will not. Pandas treats commands to divide a `DataFrame` by a `Series` as an attempt to multiply the matrix of values in the `DataFrame` by the inverse vector of the values in the `Series`. This is not the desired behavior. Rather, we must select each column of the `DataFrame` one at a time and divide it by the `Series` of text lengths. There are several ways to accomplish this, but the method here is to use `apply()` with an anonymous function.

An anonymous function is a one-line function that is defined and invoked within another line of code. It exists for as long as that line of code is executing and then is disposed of. Since it is not kept around for the next line, there is no reason to give it a name or define it before the line where it is executed. Anonymous functions are defined with the `lambda` keyword instead of `def`.

Like def, the lambda keyword is followed by one or more arguments (separated by commas). At the end of the sequence of variables is a colon, followed by one line of code to execute and return. Consider the following function.

```
def normalize(frequency_counts, text_length):
    value = frequency_counts / text_length
    return value
```

And now the equivalent anonymous function.

```
lambda frequency_counts, text_length: frequency_counts /
text_length
```

Note that lambda is used exactly as def would be (but without parentheses around the arguments) and the code to execute is separated from the def/lambda by a colon. Anonymous functions always return the result of the line of code in their body (and there cannot be more than one line of code in an anonymous function), so there is no need to include a return statement. These properties make anonymous functions ideal for use with apply().

Remember that apply() takes each column of the DataFrame and passes it into a function, which must be the first argument. This works exactly the same when the first argument is an anonymous function, so counts = counts. apply(lambda col: col / text_lengths * 1000) takes each column of counts, assigns it to the variable col, divides col by text_lengths, multiplies the result by 1,000, and returns the aggregated results of performing this operation on all columns as a DataFrame.

In step 6, subcorpora for sports reporting and all other registers are created from counts. First, the IDs of all sports reports are found using c.loc[c. register.eq('sr')].text.unique() and assigned to sr_texts. Then, these IDs are used to select only the sports reports in counts using counts.loc[sr_texts]. The same procedure is used to create a subcorpus of the non-sports reports texts using the ~ at the start of ~c. register.eq('sr') to indicate that all rows where register does *not* equal 'sr' should be selected.

In step 7, *d* values are found using apply(). As in step 5, an anonymous function is given to apply(), but the underlying logic is a bit more complex than it was in step 5. Each column of sports is passed into the anonymous function where it is assigned to the variable col. Then, col is passed to the cohen() function along with the column of others that has the same name as col.

So, for example, when the *proper nouns* column of sports is passed into the anonymous function, it, along with the *proper nouns* column in others, is passed into `cohen()`. The `cohen()` function finds the standardized mean difference between the two columns and returns it to the anonymous function, which aggregates the results of calling `cohen()` on every pair of columns in the two `DataFrames` into a single `DataFrame` and assigns it the name `results`.

One might reasonably wonder why we cannot just use `cohen()` with `apply()`. We can, but doing so would require writing the `cohen()` function to extract the appropriate column from `others`. This is possible, but creates more convoluted code than the anonymous function.

At last, in steps 8 and 9, rows with *d* values between -.2 and .2 are filtered out and the remaining values are written to a file and displayed to the console.

The results here align well with the results of Egbert and Biber (2023)'s first case study, though some magnitudes of *d* are higher in their study (proper nouns, third-person pronouns, and nominalizations). No doubt this is due to differences in operationalization of grammatical features, as well as differences in tokenization, part-of-speech tagging, and counting. The version of CORE used in their study was tokenized and tagged by the Biber Tagger (Biber & Egbert, 2018, pp. 21–22), while the dataframe version used here was tokenized and tagged using the spaCy Python package. More on tokenizing and tagging is found in Section 5.

The algorithm in this section focuses on producing per-text, normalized frequency counts for grammatical features. While the application here is KF Analysis, per-text frequencies are necessary for more complex text-linguistic procedures like multidimensional analysis as well.

Explore on your own!

1) In the preceding algorithm, premodifying nouns are operationalized as tokens with noun tags that occur in rows before tokens with noun tags. Use the concordance algorithm to examine a subset of noun-noun sequences and estimate the effectiveness of this operationalization. Can it be improved?

2) CORE is annotated with a subset of POS tags in the Penn Treebank tagset and the Universal Dependency Project tagset. Investigate these tagsets and try to write code to count gerunds, present tense verbs, and prepositional phrases. Add these to your algorithm. How do they line up with the other features?

3) Strength of association between a collocate and node can be calculated using Cohen's *d*. Create a list of collocates of *misinformation* in news by calculating the mean rate at which each word type occurs in the node word's context windows across texts and subtracting the mean

> rate at which each word type occurs outside the node word's context
> windows. Then divide by the pooled standard deviation. Compare
> these collocates to the list created using logDice. Do they overlap?
> Does one appear superior?

4.7 Conclusion

The algorithms in this section are designed with two goals in mind: to provide examples of authentic corpus linguistic analyses with Pandas dataframe corpora, and to provide a set of foundational algorithms that can be extended to novel situations, research goals, and statistical procedures. Thus far, however, we have worked exclusively with CORE. The procedures described here are not useful if they can only be applied to a handful of prebuilt corpora. The next section, therefore, describes methods for creating dataframe corpora.

5 Creating Dataframe Corpora

The examples in previous sections use a version of CORE that has already been converted to a `DataFrame`. To work with a different corpus, it is necessary to transfer it into a `DataFrame` format. This process will vary depending on file formats, metadata, and annotations.

The algorithms in this section use the spaCy natural language processing pipeline for tokenizing, part-of-speech tagging, and lemmatizing (Honnibal, 2020). It should be noted that there is some danger in reliance on third-party libraries such as spaCy (and Pandas!). The inner workings of these libraries are often hidden from the analyst who must trust that the library is producing the results that they expect. Additionally, by using these libraries, analysts lose some control over their algorithms. For example, by default, spaCy applies POS-tags from the Penn Treebank tagset, so analysts using this library must align their research goals with what is possible given that tagset. The accuracy rates (e.g., precision and recall) are also not always readily available or obscured behind averages. Arguably, however, the benefits outweigh the drawbacks. By using established, professionally written and maintained libraries, analysts not only write code in less time, but may also worry less about bugs or conceptual errors.

To create a dataframe corpus from files, it is necessary to list files in a directory, read data from those files, process and annotate these data, create a `DataFrame` for the file, and then append it to a `DataFrame` for the corpus. These four areas represent stages in a general algorithm for creating a dataframe corpus. This algorithm takes a string containing the path of the corpus as input and produces a `DataFrame` corpus from the files at that location. In the processing stage, data are read from files, tokenized and annotated, and aggregated into a single corpus `DataFrame` file.

Memory management will be a major concern when building large dataframe corpora from files. As such, it is advisable to build the corpus iteratively, one file at a time. In this approach, the first file is read, processed, and converted to a `DataFrame`. That `DataFrame` is then saved to disk in CSV format and the memory that it was occupying released. The next file is then read, processed, and appended to the file on disk. Appending to the end of a .csv file does not require Python to read the entire file into memory, so only one file at a time is taking memory resources and the only practical limit on the size of the corpus is available disk space.

At the end of this process, however, the corpus will exist as a large .csv file. For some corpora, this will be fine, but for others, the builder may want to reduce the memory footprint further by reading the corpus from the .csv file, converting the datatype of its columns to `category`, rewriting the corpus to disk in a more efficient format, and then deleting the CSV version.

Putting all this together, the general algorithm for creating a dataframe corpus from files is as follows.

Input

1. Load libraries, set constants, and create an empty `DataFrame` for the corpus.
2. Get a `list` of files to process.

Processing

3. Iterate over the `list` of files. For each file

   1. read text,
   2. tokenize and annotate the text,
   3. create a `DataFrame` for the file, and
   4. append the file `DataFrame` to the corpus `DataFrame`.

Output

4. Restructure the corpus `DataFrame` file to reduce memory requirements.

Much of the algorithm can be accomplished with functions and datatypes that have already been introduced, but not all. Some steps will vary from corpus to corpus, so the algorithm must be adapted to account for the unique characteristics of each corpus. Step 3.1, for example, will vary based on the format of the data being processed. However, so long as the data can be coerced into strings of text with no markup, the rest of the algorithm will produce fully annotated text without further modification. Similarly, step 3.2 will vary depending on the extent to which the text is already processed and annotated.

In the following sections, procedures are explained for tokenizing and annotating text using spaCy, opening and reading text from files, and listing files in a directory based on conditions. These are then combined into a single algorithm for constructing a dataframe corpus from text files. As we are constructing a new corpus, we will not use CORE in this section, but instead turn to the open portion of the American National Corpus (OANC; Ide & Suderman, 2004), which may be downloaded from www.anc.org/data/oanc/download/.

5.1 Tokenizing, POS-Tagging, and Lemmatizing with spaCy

Up-to-date instructions for installing and using spaCy may be found at https://spacy.io/. In most cases, however, users should be able to install spaCy from the command line (on a Windows computer, press Windows Key + r and then type "cmd"). Open a command-line interface and type

```
pip install spacy
```

Once spaCy (and the other packages it requires) have been installed, one or more language models must be downloaded. This can also be done at the command line using

```
python -m spacy download
```

followed by the name of the model. spaCy has several models available for many languages. We will use the *en_core_web_sm* model in the following algorithm. This model is English (*en*), one of spaCy's *core* models, trained on *web* data, and it is the small (*sm*) version. To download this model, type the following at the command line:

```
python -m spacy download en_core_web_sm
```

All code in this Element will run with spaCy version 3.0 or higher, but if pip is used to install spaCy, the most recent version available for your version of Python will be installed automatically. Similarly, if you use `python -m spacy download` to install a language model, spaCy will ensure that you have the right model installed for your version of spaCy.

With spaCy installed, it can be imported like other packages (note that the package name is lowercase despite its usual irregular capitalization).

```
import spacy
```

Before the package can be used, a language model must be loaded with `spacy.load()`. This method takes the name of a spaCy model as input (as `str`) and returns a spaCy `language` object, which we call `nlp`. Consider `nlp` a variable with properties and methods necessary to tokenize and annotate text.

```
nlp = spacy.load('en_core_web_sm')
```

We can process text by invoking `nlp` as a function and passing it a `str` with the text we wish to process. Invoking `nlp` in this way returns a spaCy `doc` (document). The doc functions like a `list` of spaCy `tokens` – one for each token in the text. Each spaCy `token` contains properties for the token itself (`text`) as well as its lemma (`lemma_`), Penn Treebank tag (`tag_`), Universal Dependency Project tag (`pos_`) and more. Consider the following code.

```
doc = nlp('Call me Jonah. '
          'My parents did, '
          'or nearly did. '
          'They called me John.')
for t in doc:
    print(t.text, t.tag_, t.lemma_)
```

```
Call VB call
me PRP I
Jonah NNP Jonah
...
My PRP$ my
parents NNS parent
did VBD do
, , ,
or CC or
nearly RB nearly
did VBD do
...
They PRP they
called VBD call
me PRP I
John NNP John
...
```

Here, we create a doc from a string using nlp. Then we iterate over doc using a for loop. On each iteration of the loop, the variable t is assigned the value of the next token in doc, and we print some of the annotations the pipeline has applied to that token. This process can be streamlined with the use of list comprehensions. All values of tag_, for example, can be extracted using

```
tags = [t.tag_ for t in doc]
tags
```

```
['VB',
'PRP',
'NNP',
'.',
'PRP$',
'NNS',
'VBD',
',',
'CC',
'RB',
'VBD',
'.',
'PRP',
'VBD',
'PRP',
'NNP',
'.']
```

A DataFrame can be constructed from a doc by extracting each type of metadata as a list and then passing those lists into the DataFrame() function as a dict with column names as keys and the lists as values.

```
tokens = [t.text for t in doc]
tags = [t.tag_ for t in doc]
lemmas = [t.lemma_ for t in doc]

c = pd.DataFrame({'token': tokens,
         'tag': tags,
         'lemma': lemmas})
c.head()
```

	token	tag	lemma
0	Call	VB	call
1	me	PRP	I

2	Jonah	NNP	Jonah
3	.	.	.
4	My	PRP$	my

This is all that is necessary for basic annotations, but spaCy provides additional types of information that may be added to the corpus, depending on the analyst's goals. Refer to https://spacy.io/api/token for more details.

5.2 Obtaining a List of Files in the Corpus

The `listdir()` function in the `os` namespace can be used to obtain a list of all the files in a directory. `listdir()` takes a string with the path of a folder as input and produces a list of strings, each of which is the name of a file in the directory. These filenames can be combined with the directory path using the `join()` function (from `os.path`). The folowing code uses a list comprehension to create a list of full paths for the files in the corpus directory.

```
filenames = listdir(path)
filepaths = [join(path, filename) for filename in filenames]
```

Here, a list of filenames is generated using `listdir()`. Then each filename is joined to the path for the root directory in the list comprehension. These two lines may alternatively be combined into a single list comprehension.

```
filepaths = [join(path, filename) for filename in listdir(path)]
```

It is also possible to only extract certain filetypes using an `if` conditional. The following code, for example, produces a list of files with `.txt` extensions (the list comprehension is broken across lines to aid readability).

```
filepaths = [join(path, filename)
    for filename in listdir(path)
    if filename.endswith('.txt')]
```

`listdir()` works when all the corpus' files are in a single folder with no nested subfolders.

```
root folder
  ↳1.txt
  ↳ file 2.txt
  ↳ file 3.txt
```

However, many corpora are stored with multiple levels of nesting.

```
root folder
  ↳ written
    ↳ fiction
      ↳ file 1.txt
      ↳ file 2.txt
```

```
↳ academic
  ↳ file 3.txt
  ↳ file 4.txt
↳ spoken
  ↳ file 5.txt
  ↳ file 6.txt
```

Getting a list of full filepaths from a directory tree like this one is more complicated, but Python provides functions for doing this. One is `walk()` in the `os` module. Consider the following code:

```
from os import walk
from os.path import join

for root, dirs, files in walk(path):
  for file in files:
    print(join(root, file))
```

The two `for` loops iterate over every file in the directory tree. It is possible, therefore, to retrieve a list of all files in the tree using a list comprehension with the same two `for` loops.

```
all_files = [join(root, file)
       for root, dirs, files in walk(path)
       for file in files]
```

Often, we want to look at every file in the directory walk, but not actually include many of them in the final list of filenames. This can be accomplished by setting conditions in the list comprehension.

```
txt_files = [join(root, file)
       for root, dirs, files in walk(path)
       for file in files
       if file.endswith('.txt')]
```

Adding `if file.endswith('.txt')` to the end of the comprehension ensures that only text files will be included in the list of filenames.

In practice, since `walk()` works in any situation and `listdir()` does not, it is generally preferable to use `walk()`. If valuable metadata about the file is in the directory structure (e.g., files containing spoken language are in a directory called `spoken`), this information can be extracted from `root`.

5.3 Creating a Corpus from Text Files

Before moving to the next algorithm, make sure you have downloaded and extracted the files of the OANC. To use the corpus, download and unpack the zip file to your working directory (the root folder should be called "data"). Note that the corpus contains text files as well as several XML files containing metadata. In the following algorithms, we will be working with only the text files. The metadata files can be used to create a second metadata `DataFrame` keyed to the texts' IDs. Doing so, however, is outside the scope of this Element.

The input is a string containing the directory where the corpus files are located, and the output is a `DataFrame` corpus. As with the general algorithm introduced at the start of this section, processing broadly involves getting a list of files and then iterating over this list – reading each file, tokenizing and annotating it, and then appending it to the corpus' `DataFrame`.

In more detail, the algorithm includes the following steps.

Input

1. `import` packages and functions.
2. Set the path to the corpus files.
3. Create spaCy `nlp`.
4. Create an empty `DataFrame`.

Processing

5. Obtain a `list` of filenames that end in *txt*.
6. Iterate over the list of filenames.

   1. Open the file and read its content into `text`.
   2. Tokenize and annotate the text using `nlp`.
   3. Extract all annotations.
   4. Create a `DataFrame` for the text.
   5. Append the text to the corpus `DataFrame`.
   6. Delete the text `DataFrame` to free resources.

7. Read the full corpus from disk; reset the categories.

Output

8. Rewrite the corpus to disk in compressed format.
9. Delete the temporary version of the corpus.

And now in Python:

```
# 1. import packages and functions
import spacy
import pandas as pd
from os import walk, remove
from os.path import join, basename
```

```
# 2. set path to data
path = "data"

# 3. create nlp
nlp = spacy.load('en_core_web_sm')

# 4. create an empty DataFrame
pd.DataFrame(columns=['token', 'type', 'lemma',
        'tag', 'pos', 'text']).\
        to_csv('temp.csv', index=False, sep='\t')

# 5. obtain a list of filenames that end in txt.
filenames = [join(root, file)
        for root, dirs, files in walk(path)
        for file in files
        if file.endswith('.txt')]

# 6. iterate over the list of filenames
for filename in filenames:

        # 6.1. open the file and read its content into text
        with open(filename, encoding='utf-8') as f:
                text = f.read()

        # 6.2. tokenize, annotate text
        doc = nlp(text)

        # 6.3. extract annotations from doc
        tokens = [t.text for t in doc]
        types = [t.text.lower() for t in doc]
        lemmas = [t.lemma_ for t in doc]
        tags = [t.tag_ for t in doc]
        poss = [t.pos_ for t in doc]
        texts = [basename(filename) for t in doc]

        # 6.4. create a DataFrame for the text
        df = pd.DataFrame({'token': tokens,
                'type': types,
                'lemma': lemmas,
                'tag': tags,
                'pos': poss,
                'text': texts}, dtype='category')
```

```
# 6.5. append the text to the corpus DataFrame
df.to_csv('temp.csv', mode='a', header=False,
    index=False, sep='\t')


# 6.6. delete the text DataFrame to free resources
del df


# 7. read the full corpus from disk; reset categories
oanc = pd.read_csv('temp.csv',
    dtype='category',
    keep_default_na=False,
    sep='\t')


# 8. write the corpus as a pickle
oanc.to_pickle('oanc.pickle')


# 9. delete the csv version of the corpus
remove('temp.csv')
```

In steps 1–3, packages are imported, the path of the root directory is set, and the spaCy `nlp` object is created. In step 4, an empty `DataFrame` is created, but not assigned to any variable. It has no rows, but columns named 'token', 'type', 'lemma', 'tag', 'pos', and 'text'. This dataframe is immediately written to a .csv file called "temp.csv". The `index` argument is set to False to prevent problems when we later append other dataframes to it. Step 5 obtains a list of files in the corpus that end in ".txt" using the `walk()` function described earlier. Step 6 begins a loop that iterates over the list of filenames.

Step 6.1 deserves additional explanation as two new features are introduced here – the `with ... as` syntax and the `open()` function. `with open(filename, encoding='utf-8') as f:` opens a file and assigns it to the variable f. `with ... as` instructs Python to open the file with a *context manager*. Context managers keep the variables they manage (specified after `as`) in memory only long enough to execute the block of code that follows the `with` statement. Using `with ... as` before the creation of f ensures that the file will be closed, and the resources allocated to it released at the end of the code block. It is a good rule of thumb to use context managers to manage variables that connect to a resource outside Python itself (e.g., databases or files). This is not necessary when we read a Pandas `DataFrame` from a file, however, because Pandas handles opening and closing connections to files.

In these lines, a context manager is used with the `open()` function to create a connection to a file. That connection is stored in the variable `f`. The text of the file is then read using `f`'s `read()` function. The argument `encoding='utf-8'` in the `open()` function tells the `read()` function to treat the data it reads as encoded with Unicode using UTF-8 (8-bit Unicode Transformation Format), a widely used, platform-independent encoding scheme.

A substantive discussion of text encoding is not desirable here; suffice it to say that a text file's encoding is the scheme that maps ones and zeros to letters, numbers, punctuation marks, emoji, and everything else. Selecting the wrong encoding may result in text artifacts or unreadable characters. It is thus crucial that the encoding scheme is properly specified for the file that is being read.

In step 6.2, the text of the file is tokenized, annotated, and stored in `doc`. Then in steps 6.3 and 6.4, the tokens and annotations are extracted and transformed into a `DataFrame`. In step 6.5, the `DataFrame` for the file is appended to the one created in step 4. The `mode='a'` argument instructs Python to append the dataframe to the end of the file instead of overwriting it (the normal behavior). As the file already contains a header (the names of the columns), `header=False` is also passed to the function to prevent it from writing new headers for each new text in the corpus. Finally, `index=False` is included as an argument to simplify aligning the full corpus later.

In step 6.6, the `DataFrame` for the text (`df`) is deleted. This frees up the memory it was occupying for the next text. Then, in steps 7 and 8, the .csv file for the full corpus is read into memory and its columns' datatypes set to `'category'`. Note that in step 7, the argument `keep_default_na=False` is passed to the `read_csv()` function. Without this argument, Pandas will treat cells in the .csv file with values such as "null", "none", and "NA" as None type data instead of words. In steps 8 and 9, the corpus is rewritten to disk as a pickle file and `temp.csv` deleted.

The corpus is now ready for use, but if you load it and examine the head, you will encounter an oddity.

```
oanc = pd.read_pickle('oanc.pickle')
oanc.head()
```

```
                      token                type \
0  \n \n \n \n            \n \n \n \n
1                        All                  all
2                        right                right
3 , ,
4                        this                 this
```

```
              lemma tag pos              text
0  \n  \n  \n  \n         _SP  SPACE Adamselissa.txt
1                   all RB   ADV  Adamselissa.txt
2                 right RB   ADV  Adamselissa.txt
3 , ,   PUNCT  Adamselissa.txt
4                  this DT   PRON  Adamselissa.txt
```

The first token in the corpus is a line of four newline characters (\n). Many of the algorithms in this Element assume that every token in the corpus is a word or punctuation mark, not whitespace. This is not an error, though. As the name suggests, spaCy retains information about whitespace when it tokenizes texts and treats some strings of whitespace as tokens. This can be useful when working with corpora where whitespace is linguistically meaningful (by e.g., delimiting speaker turns or indicating long pauses), as it is in the OANC, so it is not always desirable to filter these tokens out. If they are not useful for your analyses, however, they can be removed with

```
oanc = oanc.loc[~oanc.tag.eq('_SP')]
oanc = oanc.apply(
 lambda col: col.cat.remove_unused_categories())
oanc.to_pickle('oanc.pickle')
```

5.4 Conclusion

While the example algorithms in this section create dataframe corpora from text files, they can be applied to corpora in a wide range of common formats including data interchange formats like Java Script Object Notation (.json) and other markup languages like XML. By modifying the annotation step to use other spaCy annotations or annotations from other tools, a wide range of metadata types can be added. The basic example here is the key to creating dataframe corpora of many types.

Conclusion

Representing corpora in dataframes allows analysts to use dataframe methods to complete CL tasks. By combining these methods, it is possible to quickly produce simple, yet powerful and flexible scripts. The algorithms presented in previous sections cover several common analyses that may provide foundations for more complex tasks.

Analysts looking to go beyond the algorithms here have several options. Those interested in making their code more efficient may wish to learn more about algorithms (see, e.g., Hetland, 2014; Lee & Hubbard, 2015). Those interested in reusing algorithms or distributing their work may wish to learn more about object-oriented programming (see, e.g., Anthony, 2020). Brezina (2018) presents an excellent introduction to statistics in corpus linguistics with formulae and procedures that are readily adaptable to the algorithms in this Element.

References

Anthony, L. (2020). Programming for corpus linguistics. In M. Paquot and S. T. Gries, eds. *Practical Handbook of Corpus Linguistics*. Springer, pp. 181–207.

Biber, D., Conrad, S., & Cortes, V. (2004). If you look at . . . : Lexical bundles in university teaching and textbooks. *Applied Linguistics*, **25**(3), 371–405.

Biber, D., & Egbert, J. (2018). *Register Variation Online*. Cambridge University Press.

Brezina, V. (2018). *Statistics in Corpus Linguistics: A Practical Guide*. Cambridge University Press.

Dunning, T. E. (1993). Accurate methods for the statistics of surprise and coincidence. *Computational Linguistics*, **19**(1), 61–74.

Egbert, J., & Biber, D. (2019). Incorporating text dispersion into keyword analyses. *Corpora*, **14**(1), 77–104.

Egbert, J., & Biber, D. (2023). Key feature analysis: A simple, yet powerful method for comparing text varieties. *Corpora*, **18**(1), 121–133.

Gabrielatos, C. (2018). Keyness analysis: Nature, metrics and techniques. In C. Taylor & A. Marchi, eds. *Corpus Approaches to Discourse: A Critical Review*. Routledge, pp. 225–258.

Hetland, M. L. (2014). *Python Algorithms: Mastering Basic Algorithms in the Python Language*. Apress.

Honnibal, M., Montani, I., Van Landeghem, S., & Boyd, A. (2020). spaCy: Industrial-strength natural language processing in Python. https://spacy.io/

Ide, N., & Suderman, K. (2004, May). The American National Corpus First Release. In *Proceedings of the Fourth International Conference on Language Resources and Evaluation (LREC'04)*, Lisbon, Portugal. European Language Resources Association (ELRA). https://aclanthology.org/L04-1313/

Lee, K. D., & Hubbard, S. H. (2015). *Data Structures and Algorithms with Python*. Springer.

Nivre, J., Agić, Ž., Ahrenberg, L. et al. (2017). Universal Dependencies 2.1. https://universaldependencies.org/u/pos/

Rayson, P. (n.d.). *Log-likelihood and effect size calculator*. http://ucrel.lancs.ac.uk/llwizard.html

Rychlý, P. (2008). A lexicographer-friendly association score. Proceedings from *Recent Advances in Slavonic Natural Language Processing* (pp. 6–9). Karlova Studánka, Czech Republic: Masaryk University. nlp.fi.muni.cz/raslan/2008/raslan08.pdf

Cambridge Elements ☰

Corpus Linguistics

Susan Hunston
University of Birmingham

Professor of English Language at the University of Birmingham, UK. She has been involved in Corpus Linguistics for many years and has written extensively on corpora, discourse, and the lexis-grammar interface. She is probably best known as the author of *Corpora in Applied Linguistics* (2002, Cambridge University Press). Susan is currently co-editor, with Carol Chapelle, of the Cambridge Applied Linguistics series.

Advisory Board

Professor Paul Baker, *Lancaster University*
Professor Jesse Egbert, *Northern Arizona University*
Professor Gaetanelle Gilquin, *Université Catholique de Louvain*

About the Series

Corpus Linguistics has grown to become part of the mainstream of Linguistics and Applied Linguistics, as well as being used as an adjunct to other forms of discourse analysis in a variety of fields. It continues to become increasingly complex, both in terms of the methods it uses and in relation to the theoretical concepts it engages with. The Cambridge Elements in Corpus Linguistics series has been designed to meet the needs of both students and researchers who need to keep up with this changing field. The series includes introductions to the main topic areas by experts in the field as well as accounts of the latest ideas and developments by leading researchers.

Cambridge Elements ≡

Corpus Linguistics

Elements in the Series

For EU product safety concerns, contact us at Calle de José Abascal, 56–1°,
28003 Madrid, Spain or eugpsr@cambridge.org.

www.ingramcontent.com/pod-product-compliance
Ingram Content Group UK Ltd.
Pitfield, Milton Keynes, MK11 3LW, UK
UKHW020306140625
459647UK00006B/61